After School

Arts & Crafts
Activities

Content Development:
Jamie Gabriel

Publications International, Ltd.

Contributing Writers:
Karen E. Bledsoe, Marilee Burton, Jamie Gabriel, Kelly Milner Halls,
Kersten Hamilton, Lise Hoffman, Rita Hoppert, Ed.D., Lisa Lerner,
Suzanne Lieurance, Candyce Norvell, Stan and Shea Zukowski

Contributing Consultants:
Nancy Goodman, Susan A. Miller, Ph.D., Leslie Anne Perry, Ph.D.,
Elizabeth Crosby Stull, Ph.D.

Contributing Illustrators:
Terri and Joe Chicko, Jim Connolly, Susan Detrich, Kate Flanagan,
John Jones, Lynn Sweat

Manufactured in China.

8 7 6 5 4 3 2 1

Library of Congress Card Number: 00-109683

ISBN: 0-7853-4452-7

Contents

Beat the Boredom Blues!

Dear Parents,

After school hours often present a special challenge: How can you keep your child entertained after a long school day? *After School Arts & Crafts Activities*, that's how! This activity book offers tons of fun, interesting projects that are designed to keep children busy for hours. But the process of making arts and crafts projects is more than just busy work. Kids will also learn new skills that can be applied to school and everyday life. For example, children will learn how to take care of their arts and crafts supplies and clean up after themselves. Many of the book's projects encourage creative thinking skills, too!

Some children will be able to complete these projects with little help, but there will be times when your assistance is needed. So, it's best if you and your child review the project together and then make a decision about your role.

After School Arts & Crafts Activities is divided into six chapters:

Chapter 1 (Awesome Art Activities) offers art projects at all skill levels, including basics such as finger painting to more complex projects involving papier-mâché. This chapter is sure to help your child develop his or her artistic talents!

Chapter 2 (Cool Crafts) features projects that use familiar materials in new and often unexpected ways. While your child will enjoy all the crafts in this chapter, the tasty cooking crafts are sure to become favorites for after school snacking!

Chapter 3 (Games to Play) not only provides exciting new games to play but also shows how to make the game projects!

Chapter 4 (Celebrations!) features a world of holiday and special occasion projects. If your child is curious about the celebrations mentioned in this book, do some exploring together on the Internet or at the library to learn more.

Chapter 5 (Imagination Station) will appeal to the creative genius in your child, with projects that will allow him or her to become an inventor, write stories, design and play instruments, and a whole lot more!

Chapter 6 (Nature in the Neighborhood) reminds your child that nature is all around us, even in our own neighborhoods. Whether it's raining outside or sunny and warm, there's a nature project in this chapter that's sure to please!

Within each chapter, projects are rated according to their challenge level (see chart below). Look for the number of symbols at the beginning of each project.

🎨	Easy
🎨🎨	Medium
🎨🎨🎨	Challenging

Keep in mind that these ratings are simply a guide. The activities should be fun and enough of a challenge to be exciting for the child, however, you do not want to frustrate your child with activities that are beyond his or her skill level.

Hey, Kids . . . School's Out!

The bell signaling the end of another school day has finally rung. You're ready for a wonderful afternoon but need some new ideas to get started. Well, look no further. *After School Arts & Crafts Activities* is filled with ideas for arts and crafts projects, exciting games that you can make yourself, great gifts to make for family and friends, and even some recipes for that all-important after school snack!

Although we know you'll want to get started right away, please read these few basic steps before beginning.

- Before you begin a project, gather all your materials, remembering to ask permission first. If you need to purchase materials, take along your book, or make a shopping list so you know exactly what you need.

- Prepare your work area ahead of time, including covering any surface you work on with newspapers or an old, plastic tablecloth. Also be sure to protect your clothes by wearing an apron or a smock, especially when painting with acrylic paints. If you do get paint on your clothes, wash them with soap and warm water immediately.

- Make sure an adult is nearby to offer help if you need it. And adult help is always needed if you will be using a craft knife, an oven, a glue gun, or anything else that may be dangerous. (When using a glue gun, use the low-temperature setting.)

- Be careful not to put any materials near your mouth, and watch out for small items, such as beads, around little kids and pets. Also, keep careful watch of balloons and broken balloon pieces—they are choking hazards.

- Put away all materials and tools when you're done. Leaving a mess may mean that you hear the word "no" the next time you ask to make something!

- Have fun and be creative!

Chapter 1

Awesome Art Activities

Dot Art

This project gives a whole new meaning to dot-to-dot pictures!

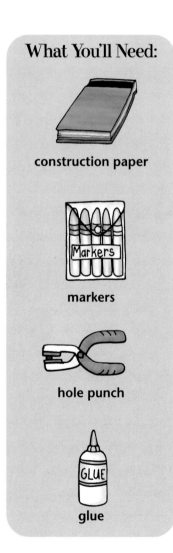

What You'll Need:

construction paper

markers

hole punch

glue

Want a new art project that is sure to keep you busy after school and makes a great gift for a family member or friend? Try Dot Art! First draw a picture on a plain sheet of white paper. Then use a hole punch to make tiny round dots from sheets of colored paper. When you punch, hold the colored paper over a different sheet of white paper to catch the dots as they fall.

Use the dots to "color" your picture by gluing them in place on different parts of your drawing. For example, if you drew a sunflower, glue green dots on the stem, yellow dots on the petals, and black dots in the middle of the flower. Be sure to leave as little white as possible without letting the dots overlap. Your finished work will have a bright, unusual look!

Corn Syrup Paint

Corn syrup paint dries with a shiny gloss.
It almost looks as if the colors are still wet!

Before you begin, be sure to cover your work surface. To make the paint, use a craft stick to mix 1 tablespoon of corn syrup with 5 or 6 drops of food coloring in 1 section of the empty egg carton. Repeat with the other colors of food coloring, keeping each paint mixture in a separate egg-carton section.

Using a black crayon, draw a design with thick outlines on a piece of heavyweight white paper. For example, if you decide to draw a baseball player, outline his pants, shirt, arms, and head with thick black crayon lines. Color in each section with the corn syrup paint. Be sure to rinse your paintbrush in water before switching colors, and don't let the colors touch one another across the black lines. This homemade paint is also great for drawing a jack-o'-lantern or Christmas tree. Since the paint is so shiny, it will seem like your pictures are all lit up!

Papier-Mâché

This pulpy mash is great for making puppet heads or adding dimension to papier-mâché projects.

What You'll Need:

newspaper

bucket of water

saucepan

spoon

colander

bowl

craft glue

dry wallpaper paste

aluminum foil

toilet paper tube

sandpaper

acrylic paints and paintbrush

Tear up 4 sheets of newspaper into stamp-size pieces. Place the newspaper pieces in a bucket of water, and soak them overnight. After the paper has soaked, have an adult boil the paper and water in a saucepan for 15 minutes. Stir the paper mixture until it is pulpy. Once the mixture has cooled, put the colander in the sink, and strain off the water. Then press on the mixture to remove any excess water. Place the paper mixture in a bowl, and add 2 tablespoons of glue and 2 tablespoons of dry wallpaper paste. Stir the mixture well until it thickens. Set the mash aside.

To make a puppet head, create a base form with crushed aluminum foil. Wrinkle and crush the foil into the head shape you want. Position the shape over the top of a toilet paper tube. Then cover the foil shape with the papier-mâché mash, and sculpt out features. Let the puppet head dry overnight. Once it's completely dry, smooth any rough edges with sandpaper, and paint the puppet head with acrylic paints.

Rubbings

*It seems like all you're doing is moving a crayon back and forth.
Then almost like magic, an object appears!*

What You'll Need:

drawing paper

leaves

crayons

scissors

GLUE
glue

Place a piece of paper over some leaves. Rub a crayon back and forth over the paper to show the texture of the leaves. Use this technique to experiment with other textured surfaces around the house, such as wood floors, tile, sandpaper, or bulletin boards. Use a different colored crayon for each surface you try.

After you have several different textures in a variety of colors, mix and match the textures on 1 piece of paper to create a textural collage. Or make personalized greeting cards out of the raised designs.

It takes more than 20 billion crayons to circle the world. If all the crayons made in a year were lined up end to end, the globe would be circled 4½ times!

Decorate a Door

Turn your bedroom door into the entrance of a magical wonderland.
All you need is paper, markers, and a little imagination!

What You'll Need:

measuring tape

scissors

butcher, wrapping, or mailing paper

markers

removable tape

old magazines (optional)

glue (optional)

Measure your bedroom door (you might need an adult to help you reach the top of the door). Cut out a rectangle the same dimensions as your door from butcher, wrapping, or mailing paper. Be sure to cut out a hole for the doorknob! Using your markers, decorate the paper any way you like. You might want to create an underwater scene, a skiing scene, or a giant "do not disturb" sign. Once you are finished decorating the paper, tape it to your door. If you don't want to draw a scene, you could make a giant collage for your door decoration. First cut out pictures of your favorite things from old magazines. Then glue them to the paper, covering the whole sheet. After the glue has dried, tape the collage to your door.

Sculpting Clay Dough

Ever wondered what a yellow elephant would look like? Or a green spaceship? Find out when you sculpt and paint your wildest fantasies.

What You'll Need:

saucepan

wooden spoon

1 cup of cornstarch

2 cups of baking soda

1¼ cups of water

waxed paper

poster paints and paintbrush

resealable plastic bag

 In a saucepan, mix cornstarch, baking soda, and water. With an adult's help, heat the mixture at a medium setting. Stir continuously until it thickens. Let the mixture cool.

Place a sheet of waxed paper over your work surface. Put the clay dough on the waxed paper, and knead the clay for a few minutes. Roll it into a ball, and shape it into small sculptures, such as animals, bugs, people—or whatever else you dream up! Let the figures air dry, then paint them with poster paints.

If you want to play with any leftover clay another day, store it in a resealable plastic bag or an airtight container, and keep it in the refrigerator.

Flower Explosion

If you thought sponges were only for cleaning up messes, you're in for a surprise with this colorful project!

What You'll Need:

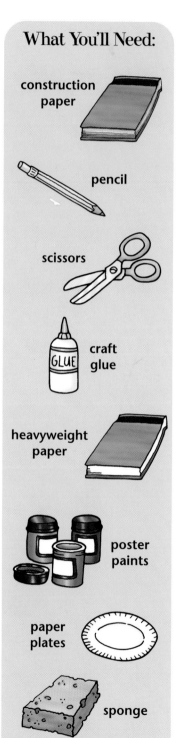

construction paper

pencil

scissors

craft glue

heavyweight paper

poster paints

paper plates

sponge

Fold a piece of construction paper in half. Draw half of a vase shape at the fold. Cut along the lines of the shape, and unfold the paper. Then glue the vase shape on a piece of heavyweight paper.

Cover your work surface, and pour poster paint colors on separate paper plates. (You'll need a paper plate for each color.) Dip a damp sponge in the paint, and then sponge paint "flowers" on the paper above the vase. Twist the sponge to create swirled flowers, or press the sponge on the paper for stamped flowers. You can make the stems and leaves by using just the corner of the sponge to draw straight lines. Be sure to rinse the sponge off with water before changing colors. You can also use this technique to make a bowl of sponged fruit, a tree with sponged leaves, or a cornucopia with sponged vegetables.

Did you know that a honeybee would have to visit more than 2 million flowers in order to collect enough nectar to produce 1 pound of honey? The bee would have to travel 55,000 miles to accomplish this feat!

Buckskin

Explore the history of Native American symbols by re-creating their beauty on pretend pelts.

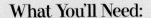

Cut a brown grocery bag in the shape of an animal's pelt. Crumple up the paper until it becomes very soft. Flatten it, then draw a buffalo, a sun and a moon, feathers, or another interesting design. Color in the picture using pastel chalks. To preserve your design, have an adult spray the paper with a very light coat of hair spray to set the chalk.

Instead of a buckskin, you could make a ceremonial shield with your pretend pelt. Cut the brown paper bag in a circle instead of a pelt shape. Crumple the paper, then flatten it and draw a Native American design on the shield. Cut out paper strips from what's left of the grocery bag to create fringe. Glue the paper strips around the circle.

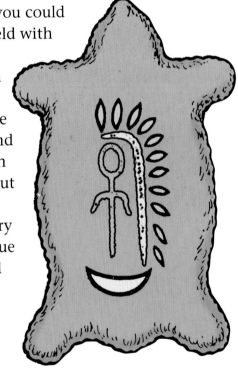

At Native American celebrations, one of the oldest and most beautiful dances for women is called the Ladies' Buckskin. A well-dressed Buckskin dancer will usually wear clothing from head to toe made almost entirely of buckskin!

Framed Art

This project gives your artwork a finishing touch.
You'll be just like a professional artist in a real gallery!

What You'll Need:

precut colored mat (available at art supply stores; find the size to fit your artwork)

assorted shapes of dry pasta

glitter

sequins

craft glue

magnetic strips

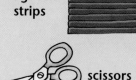

scissors

  Decorate the mat with assorted shapes of pasta, glitter, and sequins. Glue them on the frame in a random design; let the glue dry. Cut 4 magnetic strips to fit the 4 sides of the mat. Glue 1 strip on each side on the back of the mat. Use this decorated mat to frame your drawings on the refrigerator. Change your picture as often as you like.

Did you know that Winslow Homer, a famous artist of the 19th century, was banned from some museums because he would try to add more detail to or touch up his paintings after they were already framed and on display?

Shades of Color

One color can be quite interesting. Just add a little white or black paint to create different tones.

What You'll Need:

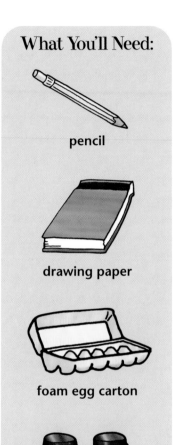

pencil

drawing paper

foam egg carton

poster paints and paintbrush

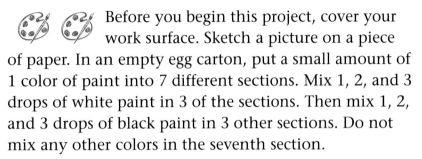 Before you begin this project, cover your work surface. Sketch a picture on a piece of paper. In an empty egg carton, put a small amount of 1 color of paint into 7 different sections. Mix 1, 2, and 3 drops of white paint in 3 of the sections. Then mix 1, 2, and 3 drops of black paint in 3 other sections. Do not mix any other colors in the seventh section.

Now paint your picture using the color and the various tones of that color. For example, if your picture is a baseball game and the color you chose is green, you can paint the scene in shades of green: dark green stands, light green uniforms, and medium green grass. Think about the direction the sun might shine on the field. Place lighter shades facing the light and darker shades away from the light to make shadows.

Toothpick Architecture

Create a tiny city, geometric shapes, or a circus tent with clowns—all out of toothpicks! You can build whatever your imagination dreams up.

What You'll Need:

waxed paper

plastic-based clay

toothpicks

poster board

Place a sheet of waxed paper over your work surface. Roll the plastic-based clay into several ¼- to ½-inch balls. The number of balls will depend on what you're making, since the clay balls are the anchor joints of your toothpick creation. For example, to make a person, you might use 7 balls of clay; to make a building, you could use 14 balls; and to make a triangle shape, you might need 4 balls of clay. (If you want a permanent structure, use the Sculpting Clay Dough on page 11.)

Insert a toothpick into a ball of clay. Then connect the toothpick to another ball of clay. Continue connecting toothpicks with the clay balls until you have completed your structure. Place the finished projects on a piece of poster board to display your creations.

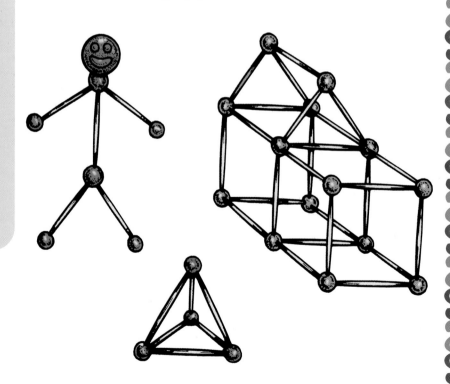

Brayer Printing

A brayer evenly applies paint to large areas without brush lines.
Learn how a brayer works—and make a cool design in the process!

What You'll Need:

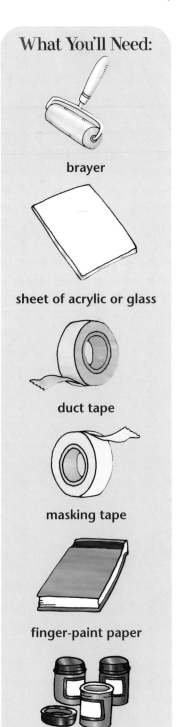

brayer

sheet of acrylic or glass

duct tape

masking tape

finger-paint paper

poster paints

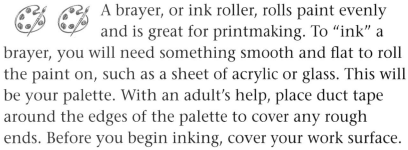 A brayer, or ink roller, rolls paint evenly and is great for printmaking. To "ink" a brayer, you will need something smooth and flat to roll the paint on, such as a sheet of acrylic or glass. This will be your palette. With an adult's help, place duct tape around the edges of the palette to cover any rough ends. Before you begin inking, cover your work surface.

Place pieces of masking tape across a sheet of finger-paint paper to create a stripe design. Then put 3 dots of different colored paint on the end of the palette in a row. Place the brayer on the paint dots, and roll along the palette to coat the brayer with the 3 colors. Then roll the inked brayer over the paper to make a stripe design. When the paint is dry, peel off the tape to find yet another pattern!

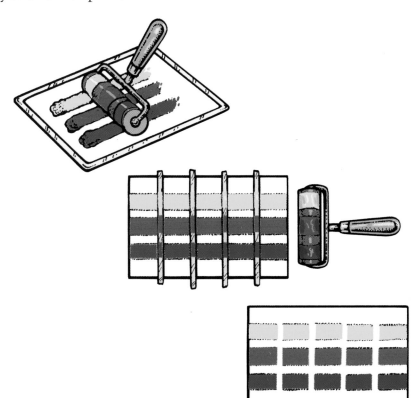

Hardware Sculpture

Nail down a cool metal sculpture with this fun and unusual activity.

As hard as it is to believe, you can make a great sculpture with nothing more than nuts, bolts, screws, and other hardware. Ask your parents to go through their spare hardware, or go to a hardware store to get started. Pick out a good-size washer, some tiny nails, drapery hooks, and anything else that captures your imagination.

Have an adult help you glue the hardware together using household cement. (Be sure the room is well-ventilated, and keep the cement out of your eyes.) Want to make a ladybug? Try a washer with 6 tiny nail legs and miniature nut eyes. A spider? Have an adult help you bend 8 long nails and attach them to a washer, with a rounded nut for the spider's silvery head. You're only limited by your supplies and your imagination!

Poster Redesign

Take an old poster, and make it brand new.
All you have to do is let your imagination run wild!

What You'll Need:

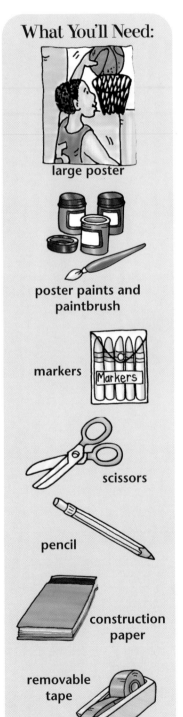

large poster

poster paints and paintbrush

markers

scissors

pencil

construction paper

removable tape

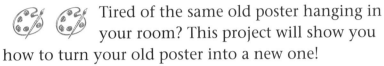 Tired of the same old poster hanging in your room? This project will show you how to turn your old poster into a new one!

Maybe you want to make Michael Jordan play football. First, cover your work surface. Then paint a football helmet and uniform on Michael. Or you could make a poster of puppies into a poster of out-of-this-world space aliens. Use markers to draw antennae on the puppies, spaceships in space, and stars in the sky.

Once you've finished making your "new" poster, hang it on your wall, or use it as a game for your next party. You can play pin the helmet on Michael or pin the antenna on the space-alien puppies. Draw helmet or antenna shapes on construction paper. Cut them out, and use them as the game pieces to "pin" on the poster with removable tape.

The Art of Tracing

Tracing an object is just the beginning. The fun comes when you color it in using your imagination and wild designs.

What You'll Need:

old magazines

scissors

lightweight
white paper

clear tape

black felt-tip pen

colored pencils

You can trace any picture without tracing paper. Pick a picture from a magazine that you want to trace, and cut it out. Tape the picture with a piece of lightweight paper over it on a window. You'll be able to see the outline of the picture through the paper. Use a black felt-tip pen to trace the outline of the picture. Take the picture and paper off the window.

Next, add your own details to the outline, and color it in. If you traced a picture of a dog, draw and color in the eyes, the nose, the fur—or whatever else you want to add. Another idea is to turn the shape you traced into something else. For example, you could use the outline of a dog to make a monster or a space alien instead!

Sugar Cube Sculptures

Sugar is sweet—but it can also be art!

What You'll Need:

cardboard

scissors

markers

sugar cubes

thick poster paints and paintbrush

glue

These sugar cube sculptures will make a unique present for someone you think is sugary sweet! Start by cutting out a square or circle of cardboard to make the base for your sculpture. You can write a message to the person you are giving the sculpture to on this base.

Next, cover your work area. Paint sugar cubes in a variety of colors; let them dry. Then glue the cubes together to make interesting shapes on top of the base. You might want to build a little sugar cube house or castle, or stack the sugar cubes in a pattern of repeating colors. Think about who you are giving your sculpture to, and let thoughts of them guide your imagination to create a truly original work of art. (Don't eat the sugar cubes. They are for your art project, not for eating!)

Palette Painting

This technique uses dabs and dots of paint instead of straight lines, adding dimension to your artwork.

What You'll Need:

foam egg carton

cornstarch

poster paints

craft stick

cardboard

 In a section of your egg carton, use a craft stick to mix a small amount of cornstarch with a color of poster paint until the mixture becomes thick like pudding. Repeat in other sections of the egg carton with other colors of paint. (Be sure to rinse off your craft stick before mixing another color.)

Now "paint" a picture on a piece of cardboard. Use a craft stick to apply the thick paint to the cardboard. The paint will stick up from your paper, creating a cool, 3-D look. Make heavy areas of color by building up the thick paint; to make light areas of color, spread out the paint. Try an abstract design first. Then try to paint a portrait of someone. Don't get frustrated— since you are painting with a craft stick, you won't be able to add a lot of detail.

Famous American artist Norman Rockwell found success with his palette at an early age. He was only a teenager when he was hired as art director of Boy's Life, the official magazine of the Boy Scouts of America.

Sculpting Clay Statues

The main difference between a good sculptor and a great sculptor is imagination. So let yourself go wild!

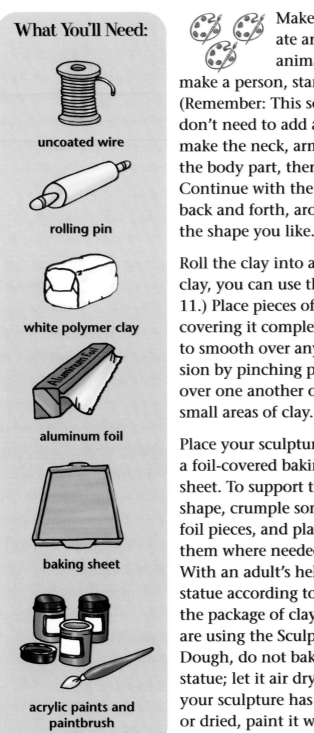

What You'll Need:

- uncoated wire
- rolling pin
- white polymer clay
- aluminum foil
- baking sheet
- acrylic paints and paintbrush

 Make a wire base for your clay statue. Create any shape you want—a person, an animal, or even a common object. To make a person, start by twisting the wire to make a face. (Remember: This sculpture can be a bit abstract, so you don't need to add a lot of detail.) Next, move down to make the neck, arms, and body. First make the line of the body part, then make loopy twists of wire around it. Continue with the rest of the figure, looping the wire back and forth, around and around, until the figure has the shape you like.

Roll the clay into a thin pancake. (Instead of polymer clay, you can use the Sculpting Clay Dough on page 11.) Place pieces of clay over the wire shape, covering it completely. Use your fingers to smooth over any gaps. Add dimension by pinching patches of clay over one another or cutting away small areas of clay.

Place your sculpture on a foil-covered baking sheet. To support the shape, crumple some foil pieces, and place them where needed. With an adult's help, bake the clay statue according to directions on the package of clay. (If you are using the Sculpting Clay Dough, do not bake the statue; let it air dry.) After your sculpture has cooled or dried, paint it with acrylic paints.

Scratch Board

Etch in a design on Scratch Board to see the contrast between dramatic black and bold brights. Your picture will look like it's jumping off the paper!

What You'll Need:

poster board

crayons

small dish

craft stick

dish soap

black poster paint and paintbrush

toothpick

First, cover your work surface. Then color a piece of poster board with crayons in assorted colors, covering the board completely with a thick layer of color. Next, use a craft stick to mix black poster paint and 2 drops of dish soap together. Use the mixture to paint over the layer of crayons. Let the paint dry completely.

Once the paint is dry, make a design or a picture by scratching off the black paint with a toothpick. The bright crayon colors will burst right through the black paint!

Leonardo da Salty

Use science and salt to make amazing pictures!

What You'll Need:

warm water

salt

plastic cups

spoon

food coloring

heavyweight paper

paintbrushes

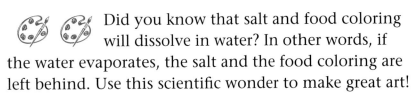 Did you know that salt and food coloring will dissolve in water? In other words, if the water evaporates, the salt and the food coloring are left behind. Use this scientific wonder to make great art!

Before you begin, cover your work surface. Mix warm water and salt together in several plastic cups. Add as much salt to each solution as it will hold—until no more salt will dissolve. Add a few drops of different food coloring to each container, and mix well.

Now, paint a picture on paper using the colored salt solutions. Put it on thick so that when it dries, a lot of salt will be left behind. Let the painted paper sit for several hours until the water evaporates, and then observe. Notice how the color and salt remain on the paper. The interesting patterns of color around the salt crystals create a beautiful picture.

Foam Tray Casting

Look around your house for small, flat objects, and reproduce their shapes to make paperweights and pretty plaques.

What You'll Need:

tools (craft knife, cookie cutters, keys, screws)

clean foam meat tray

plaster of Paris

mixing bowl

spoon

acrylic paints and paintbrush

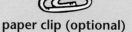

paper clip (optional)

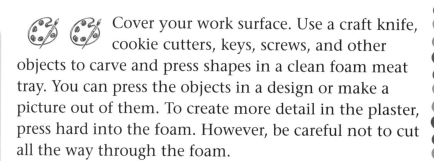 Cover your work surface. Use a craft knife, cookie cutters, keys, screws, and other objects to carve and press shapes in a clean foam meat tray. You can press the objects in a design or make a picture out of them. To create more detail in the plaster, press hard into the foam. However, be careful not to cut all the way through the foam.

Have an adult help you mix the plaster of Paris according to package directions. Carefully pour the plaster in the foam tray. (Be sure to throw unused plaster away. Do not pour it down the sink; it will clog the pipes.) If you'd like to hang your plaster casting, press a paper clip into the top edge of the mold. Let the plaster set. When it's dry, pop it out of the tray. Add color to your plaster casting with acrylic paints.

Pencil Painting

Draw a picture, then turn it into a painting with these "magic" pencils.

What You'll Need:

water-soluble colored pencils (available at art supply stores)

drawing paper

paintbrush

water

Draw a lion on a sheet of drawing paper using yellow and brown water-soluble colored pencils. (They feel and look just like regular colored pencils.) Add big green eyes to your lion and other details to make your picture come to life. Then wash over your picture using a damp paintbrush. (Be sure to clean your paintbrush when you change from blending one color to another color.) The colors blend just like watercolor paints!

Water scenes are also fun to paint using these "magic" pencils. Draw a boat at a pier by the lake, using blue pencils for the water. Then use the blending technique to create the boat's reflection in the water. Experiment with other scenes and colors.

Self-Portraits

If a close friend or grandparent lives far away, send a self-portrait to them. It's better than a photograph!

What You'll Need:

grocery bags

scissors

masking tape

markers

yarn and fabric scraps
(optional)

Cut up 2 or 3 grocery bags, then tape them together end to end. Place the paper on the floor, and tape it down to hold it in place. Lie down on the paper, and have a friend or family member trace around your body. Now decorate your outline with markers. If you want, glue on yarn for your hair and fabric scraps for your clothes. Make yourself into anything you want. You can be yourself, an astronaut, or a ballerina. Mail your self-portrait to a friend or family member who lives far away—they'll be thrilled to receive a picture of you, made by you!

Double Drawing

This project will make you think you're seeing double!

Hold 2 crayons side by side, and tape them together. You can tape together two of the same color or 2 different colors. Now draw a picture with the 2 crayons on a piece of drawing paper. Your picture will have double lines. Write your name a few times, or make the same design, such as a heart, over and over in different colors and sizes. Change color combinations often.

After you've finished drawing your picture, color the spaces in between the lines to create a bold design. You could even color in the spaces using watercolor paints to create a resist effect, which makes the lines stand out.

Identical twins are perhaps the world's most noticeable pairs. But not everything about them is duplicated. According to Los Angeles forensics experts, the perfect resemblance stops when it comes to fingerprints.

Foil Embossing

Whether you emboss one pretty flower or a wild abstract design, these wall hangings will shine in any room.

What You'll Need:

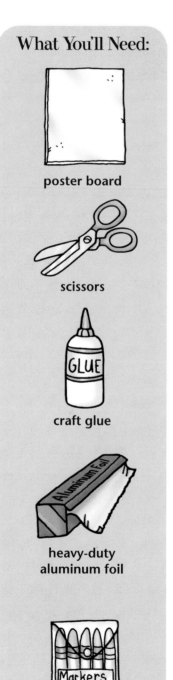

poster board

scissors

craft glue

heavy-duty
aluminum foil

permanent
markers

Cut 2 pieces of poster board into the size of the picture you want to make. These will be your backing pieces. It's best to start with small pieces, about 8×10 inches. Then cut out some geometric shapes from poster board. Glue them in a design on one of the poster board backing pieces. For example, you could create an abstract geometric design or arrange triangle shapes into a pinwheel or square shapes into a checkerboard.

After the glue has dried, place a piece of heavy-duty foil over the top of the shapes, and rub the foil with your fingers until the design is raised onto the foil. Leave the foil in place, and color the raised design with permanent markers. Carefully remove the foil, and glue it on the other poster board backing piece.

Acrylic on Acrylic

Doing your homework won't seem so bad when you're working at a desk covered in your very own artwork!

 Be sure to cover your work surface before you begin this project. Use a grease pencil to draw a design on the sheet of acrylic. You could create a theme to match your room, hobbies, or interests, or just draw a pretty picture.

Turn the acrylic sheet over on your work surface with the drawing side down. Using the grease pencil outlines as your guide, fill in the design with acrylic paints. (If you color outside the lines, it really doesn't matter. They're your guide for coloring in the design, and you'll erase the lines when you're done anyway.) Start painting in the middle of the sheet first, then work toward the edges. Let the paint dry. Then turn the sheet over, and wipe off the grease pencil using a paper towel. Place the acrylic sheet on your desk, paint side down.

Crewel Burlap

You probably know that artwork can be drawn with pen, pencil, or paint. But did you know you can also draw with yarn?

What You'll Need:

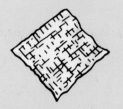

craft burlap (available at craft or fabric stores)

markers

assorted colors of yarn

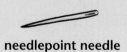

needlepoint needle

 Draw a picture on a piece of burlap with markers. For example, you could make a picture of a garden with a scarecrow and a line of crows sitting on a split-rail fence. Using your marker outline, sew yarn around the picture in long and short stitches. Go in and out with a needlepoint needle using different colors of yarn to match what you are outlining. You can even fill in areas by going back and forth with the yarn. Pick small areas that need emphasizing to fill in your picture, such as the black crows and the scarecrow's face.

In Japan, the scarecrow is considered to be the god of farms. In fact, there is a festival in October called Kakashi-age to thank them for watching over the harvest.

Sculpting Cookies

The dough starts out looking like real clay, but after it's baked, there's no doubt these sculptures are a sweet treat!

What You'll Need:

mixing bowl

spoon

½ cup of peanut butter

2 tablespoons of honey

1 egg

¾ cup of flour

½ teaspoon of baking soda

waxed paper

cookie sheet

 Mix the peanut butter, honey, egg, flour, and baking soda together in a mixing bowl. Place a sheet of waxed paper on your work surface, and sprinkle a bit of flour over the waxed paper. Knead the dough on the floured waxed paper, then pinch and shape the dough as if it were clay. Sculpt it into simple objects like a worm, snail, or ladybug, or form the dough into letters of the alphabet.

Once you've formed your sculptures, place them on an ungreased cookie sheet. Have an adult help you bake the cookies at 350 degrees Fahrenheit for 8 to 10 minutes. Let them cool, then serve your sweet sculptures to family and friends!

To celebrate the New Year in Tibet, elaborate yak-butter sculptures are created to represent a special story or fable. The sculptures reach 30 feet high and are lit with special butter lamps. Awards are given for the best sculptures!

Kitchen Collection Art

It's hard to believe that such an interesting picture started out as odds and ends headed for the garbage can!

What You'll Need:

plastic cup

markers

collection of throwaway items (bottle caps, string, screws)

craft glue

poster board

Place a plastic cup in the kitchen to collect all kinds of throwaway, nonfood items. Label your cup "Kitchen Collection Cup" so that everyone knows to put the items in the cup. Once the cup is full, take a look at what you have collected. Arrange and glue the objects into an interesting collage on a piece of poster board. You'll have so much fun collecting the items that you may want to put a cup in the laundry room and your bedroom for other kinds of objects.

Americans produce a lot of garbage. The city of San Francisco alone has to dispose of 5 million pounds of garbage every day! That's equal in weight to 3,000 elephants!

Paper Weaving

Go ahead! Make waves as well as zigzags and curves—all with one fun and colorful paper-weaving technique.

What You'll Need:

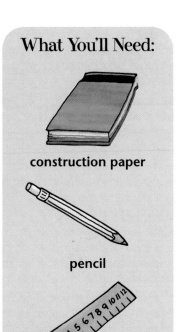

construction paper

pencil

ruler

scissors

craft glue (optional)

Measure and mark several 1-inch strips lengthwise on a piece of construction paper. Cut out the strips, and repeat these steps with several different colors of paper. Fold another piece of construction paper in half. Starting at the fold, cut straight lines about 1 inch apart to 1 inch from the edge of each side of the paper. Open the paper, and weave each paper strip over and under each cut. Alternate colors of strips as you weave. Continue weaving until the paper is full. Trim the strips, and glue ends in place. If you want, glue your paper weaving on a larger piece of paper, and hang it on a wall for all to see!

Weaving is one of the very oldest art forms. Early weavers in India, working without any tools, joined grasses with interlacing leaves to form special woven mats. These grass mats were used for religious purposes like sitting down to pray or meditate.

Chapter 2

Cool Crafts

Beauty in a Bottle

A sand painting in a bottle makes a nice gift.
It's also fun to make a collection of them in different-size bottles.

What You'll Need:

jar

colored sand
(available at
craft stores)

Find a nice-looking jar that has a cork or a cap. Fill the jar with layers of different-colored sand to make a design.

Here are some ideas to try: Alternate thin layers and thick layers, or repeat color patterns. For example, layer red, orange, and yellow; then repeat the pattern. Or you could make wavy stripes by tilting the bottle while you add sand. When the bottle is full, put the cap on. If you don't have colored sand, you can use different textures of sand (coarse and fine) or even sand and pebbles.

In Tibet, sand painting by Buddhist monks is considered a sacred art. Millions of grains of colored sand are carefully laid out on a flat platform to produce beautiful works of art. When finished, the sand is swept into a nearby river to carry away the healing power of the sand painting!

Clay Accessories

Create jewelry for your hair by making this beautiful and very special barrette.

What You'll Need:

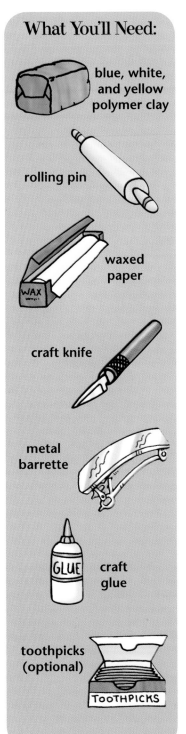

blue, white, and yellow polymer clay

rolling pin

waxed paper

craft knife

metal barrette

craft glue

toothpicks (optional)

  Roll out a thin, even pancake of blue clay on waxed paper. Using a craft knife, cut the blue clay into a rectangle slightly larger than your metal barrette. Knead or roll out a small amount of white and yellow clay on waxed paper. Use your craft knife to cut out tiny stars and a moon from the white and yellow clay. Place them on the blue clay piece. Bend the clay to match the curve of the barrette. With an adult's help, bake the clay according to package directions. After the clay piece has cooled, glue it to the back of the barrette.

You can also make your own buttons from clay. After you've rolled out the clay, just cut out small circles for buttons. Use toothpicks to punch 2 holes in the middle of each circle, decorate the buttons with other pieces of clay, and bake. After the clay has cooled, sew the buttons on your favorite shirt. (Once baked, the clay buttons can be machine-washed and dried on the gentle cycle.)

Cereal Box Bookbinding

*Create your own journal, scrapbook, or sketchbook
to have a place for your precious memories.*

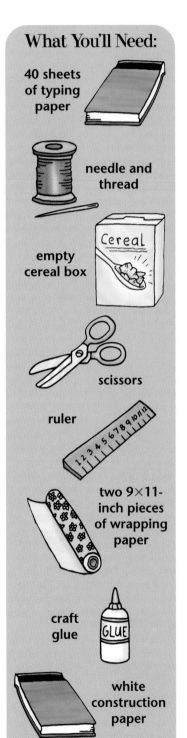

What You'll Need:

40 sheets of typing paper

needle and thread

empty cereal box

scissors

ruler

two 9×11-inch pieces of wrapping paper

craft glue

white construction paper

 Fold 40 sheets of typing paper in half. Separate 8 sheets from the 40, and sew the pages together along the fold using a needle and thread. Repeat with 4 more 8-page sections. Then cut out the front and back covers from a cereal box. Follow the cut lines shown in the illustration on the right to make two 6×9-inch pieces with a ½-inch spine.

Wrapping paper

Place a 9×11-inch piece of wrapping paper on your work surface, and cut off the corners as shown. Coat the front cover piece with glue, and place it down on the wrapping paper. Glue the flaps over. Repeat for the back cover.

Cut white construction paper into two 5×7-inch pieces. Glue 1 piece to the inside of each cover. Glue the spines of the front and back covers together. Then put glue on the inside spine, and insert the five 8-page sections. Let it set overnight.

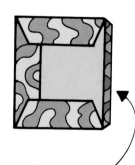

Spine

Shadow Puppets

Even with all the lights on, these funny shadow shapes stay around to play some more.

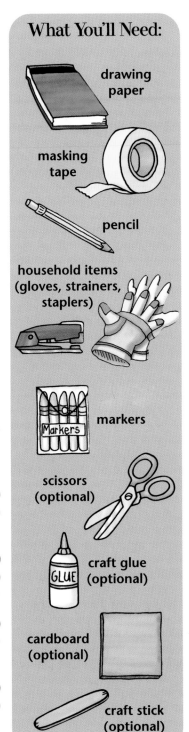

What You'll Need:

drawing paper

masking tape

pencil

household items (gloves, strainers, staplers)

markers

scissors (optional)

craft glue (optional)

cardboard (optional)

craft stick (optional)

Pick out a room with a light-colored wall. Turn on a lamp, and practice making shadows on the wall with your hands. Try crossing your thumbs over one another and spreading your fingers apart to make a bird. Or hold 1 hand sideways with your thumb on top and your pinky at the bottom to make a dog.

When you're done practicing, tape a piece of paper on the wall. Make a shadow puppet on the paper, and have a friend draw an outline around the shape. Use household items such as gloves, strainers, and staplers to make more shadow puppets. Take turns with your friend making shapes and drawing outlines until you have a whole zoo. Color in your animal shapes with markers.

To make your shapes into stick puppets, cut out an animal shape, and glue it on a piece of cardboard. Cut

Personalize Your Hats

Turn an old baseball cap into a new, stylish hat of your own.
The possibilities are endless!

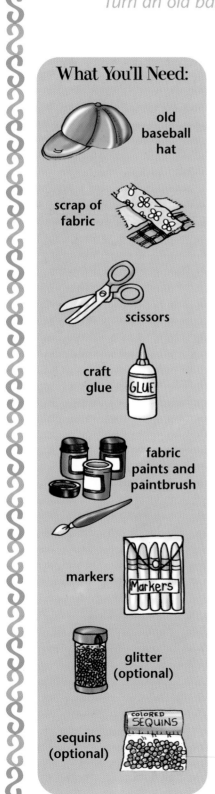

What You'll Need:

- **old baseball hat**
- **scrap of fabric**
- **scissors**
- **craft glue**
- **fabric paints and paintbrush**
- **markers**
- **glitter (optional)**
- **sequins (optional)**

Cut out a circle or square from a scrap of fabric that is large enough to cover the front emblem of your baseball hat. Glue the fabric over the emblem. Then decorate your hat with fabric paints and markers.

Need ideas? How about turning your baseball hat into a fun beach cap? Paint an underwater ocean scene with fish and seaweed. Let the paint dry, then use the markers to add detail to the picture. You could also glue on glitter and sequins to make the fish sparkle.

Many words and phrases connected with hats have become part of everyday language. You "hold onto your hat" by staying calm when you're feeling excited. When you're working out a problem, you "put on your thinking cap." If you want to compliment someone, you say, "hats off to you!" Can you think of any other examples?

Clay Printer

*Print a special message or a unique design
with your very own printing block.*

What You'll Need:

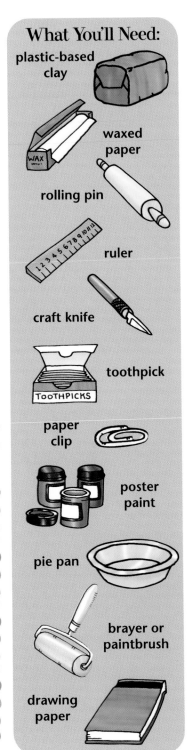

plastic-based clay

waxed paper

rolling pin

ruler

craft knife

toothpick

paper clip

poster paint

pie pan

brayer or paintbrush

drawing paper

 Roll out an even pancake of clay about ¼ inch thick on waxed paper. Use a craft knife to cut the clay into a 3×5-inch rectangle. Then sketch a design on the clay using a toothpick. If you are using letters in your design, write them backward. (The design will be the raised part of the clay that will print.) Use the craft knife and a paper clip to scrape away clay from the design so that it is raised.

Pour poster paint into a pie pan, and roll a brayer in the paint. Using the brayer, cover the clay piece with paint. If you don't have a brayer, paint the raised part of the clay with a paintbrush.

Now lay a piece of drawing paper over the painted clay. Press gently to imprint your design on the paper. If you want to use a different color, carefully rinse the paint off the Clay Printer, and repaint it with the brayer to make another print. Once the paint is dry, you can use your printed pieces to make wrapping paper, notecards, or even a wall picture.

Fabric Fruit

*Fabric Fruit makes a pretty table decoration,
especially when you put it in a handmade bowl.*

What You'll Need:

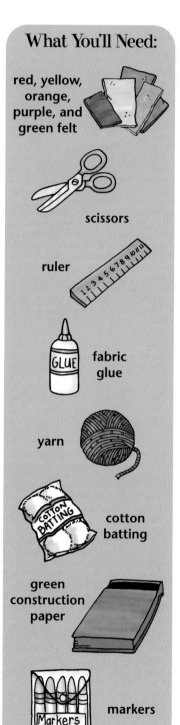

red, yellow, orange, purple, and green felt

scissors

ruler

fabric glue

yarn

cotton batting

green construction paper

markers

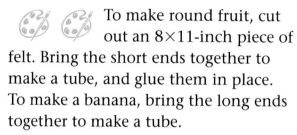 To make round fruit, cut out an 8×11-inch piece of felt. Bring the short ends together to make a tube, and glue them in place. To make a banana, bring the long ends together to make a tube.

Twist 1 end of the tube, and tie it closed with yarn.

Turn the fabric inside out. Then stuff it with cotton batting. Twist the other end of the tube, and tie it with yarn to close it.

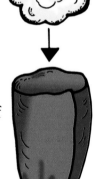

 Cut a leaf shape from a piece of green construction paper. Tuck 1 end of the leaf into the yarn. If you want, draw decorations on your fruit with markers. Make more round fruit with different colors of fabric, and arrange them in a bowl.

Cookies on a Stick

These cookies are as much fun to make as they are to eat!

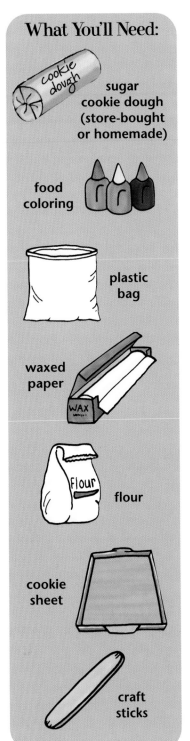

What You'll Need:

sugar cookie dough (store-bought or homemade)

food coloring

plastic bag

waxed paper

flour

cookie sheet

craft sticks

Divide the cookie dough into 3 or 4 balls. Add a different color of food coloring to each ball, then knead the dough balls to mix in the colors. Place the dough in a plastic bag, and chill it in the refrigerator for 1 hour.

Cover your work surface with waxed paper, and sprinkle it with a bit of flour. Roll a piece of dough into a round pancake. Then roll pieces of dough into balls and strips. Use the strips and balls of dough to add features on the pancake. For example, you could make a funny face or an animal character. Make as many cookies as you can out of the dough. Then place the cookies on a cookie sheet, and insert a craft stick into the bottom edge of each cookie. With an adult's help, bake the cookies according to the package or recipe directions.

Special Seed Bracelets

*Let the world see your friendship when you and
a friend wear these matching bracelets.*

What You'll Need:

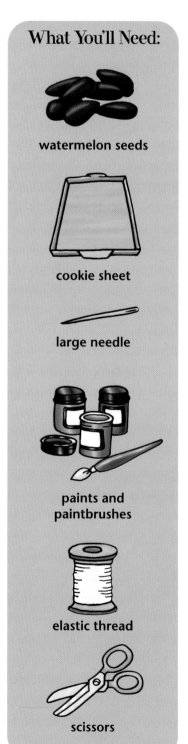

watermelon seeds

cookie sheet

large needle

paints and
paintbrushes

elastic thread

scissors

Wash lots of watermelon seeds. (Use the dark brown seeds; the white ones may not be firm enough.) Spread the seeds out on a cookie sheet, and let them dry overnight. When they are dry, have an adult help you carefully poke a hole through the top of each seed with a large needle.

Cover your work surface. To make matching bracelets, decide with your friend what colors you should paint the seeds. You might want to use both of your favorite colors, alternating them when you thread the seeds on the elastic. Or you could draw dots or tiny hearts on your seeds. Use your imagination! When you paint the seeds, paint 1 side, and let the paint dry. Then turn the seeds over, and paint the other side.

Once the paint is dry on both sides, thread the seeds onto enough elastic to make a bracelet. Knot the elastic. You and your friend can then slip your bracelets onto your wrists and declare your friendship to be forever!

Childhood Home

You'll always remember the place where you grew up when you look at this homey model.

What You'll Need:

construction paper

clear tape

scissors

glue

old home decorating magazines and catalogs

markers

To create a model of your childhood home, fold in 2 sides of a large sheet of construction paper to meet at the middle, so that each side opens and closes. You might need to tape a few sheets together to get a piece that is large enough. Cut a triangle-shape roof for your house, and glue it to the top of the flaps of the closed house. (If you live in an apartment building, you might not have a roof like this.) Cut up from the bottom of the triangle to the point so the roof will open and close with the flaps. Cut out and glue on a chimney as well.

Find pictures of doors, windows, trees, flowers, and other details in old home decorating magazines and catalogs. Cut these out, and glue them to the outside of your house. Then open your house, and divide it into the number of rooms that are in your home. Cut out furnishings from the magazines, and glue them in the rooms where they belong. Find rugs, beds, tables, chairs, curtains, and plants that look similar to things you have in your house. You can change the color of objects with markers. As you get older, you will always want to remember this special place where you shared so much with your loved ones.

Dream Catcher

Make all your good dreams come true!

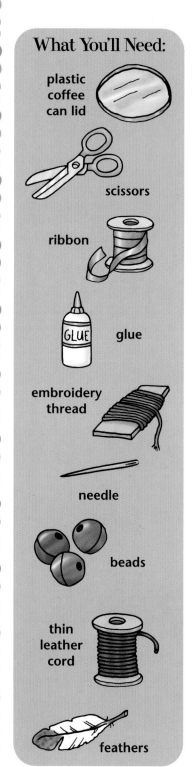

What You'll Need:

plastic coffee can lid

scissors

ribbon

glue

embroidery thread

needle

beads

thin leather cord

feathers

Cut out the middle of a plastic coffee can lid to make a ring. You may need an adult's help for this part. Wind the ribbon several times around the ring until it is totally covered and nicely padded, then glue the ends in place. Loosely wrap embroidery thread around the plastic ring to form 8 small loops. Use a needle to weave the thread in and out of the loops around the ring. Loosely knot the thread to each loop. Then sew each loop with its opposite loop to make a web. Hold a bead in the center, and pass the thread through it each time you sew 2 loops together.

To finish, tie loops of thin leather cord to the top and bottom of the ring. Cut the bottom loop so 2 lengths of cord hang down. Thread beads and glue feathers to these ends. Hang the Dream Catcher over your bed using the top loop. According to tradition, all your bad dreams will get caught in the web, but all your good dreams will pass through the center and come true!

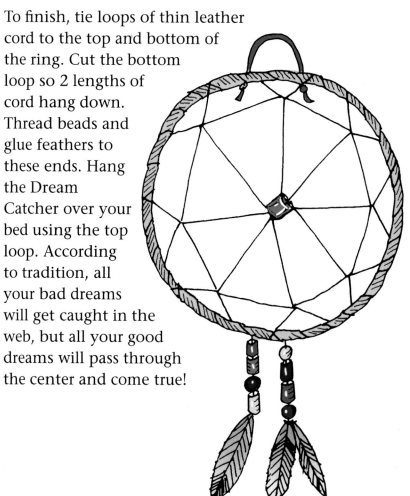

Stained-Glass Vase

Hate to throw away those neat-looking glass bottles that hold water or iced tea? Make beautiful vases with them!

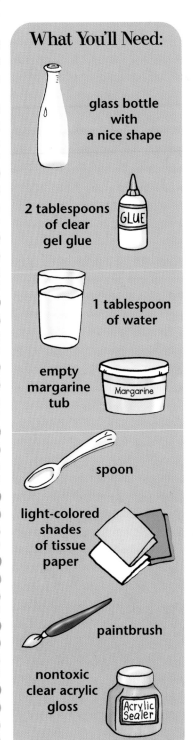

What You'll Need:

glass bottle with a nice shape

2 tablespoons of clear gel glue

GLUE

1 tablespoon of water

empty margarine tub

Margarine

spoon

light-colored shades of tissue paper

paintbrush

nontoxic clear acrylic gloss

Acrylic Sealer

Start by removing all the labels and metal rings from the bottle. Then wash and dry it thoroughly. Cover your work surface. In a clean, empty margarine tub, mix together clear gel glue and water. Tear off pieces of tissue paper about the size of a quarter. Then brush some of the glue mixture on the bottle in a patch the size of a quarter. Lay a piece of tissue paper on that part of the bottle. Now hold the piece down with your thumb while lightly brushing glue on top of the paper. Add 1 piece at time, slightly overlapping the edges. Work carefully! Finish covering the bottle (you only need 1 layer), then fold some tissue paper over the lip of the bottle all the way around. Layer pieces under the bottom edge of the bottle, too. Let dry for a day. Coat the bottle with clear acrylic gloss, according to package directions. Let dry. Add some flowers, and admire what a sunlit window does for your vase!

Bath Jelly

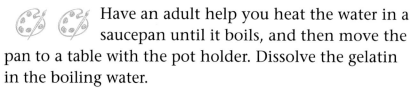

Here's a cool concoction to create in your scientific laboratory (also known as your kitchen)! Use the Bath Jelly yourself, or give it to someone as a gift.

What You'll Need:

½ cup of water

saucepan

pot holder or oven mit

1 envelope of unflavored gelatin

Gelatin

spoon

½ cup of bubble bath or liquid soap

Dish Soap

food coloring

jar with lid

small toy or seashells

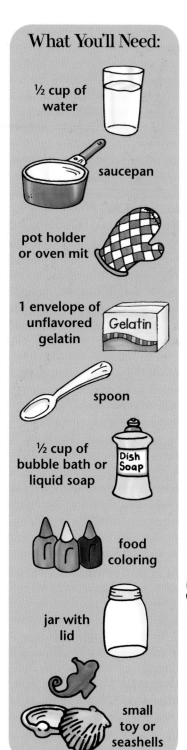

Have an adult help you heat the water in a saucepan until it boils, and then move the pan to a table with the pot holder. Dissolve the gelatin in the boiling water.

When the gelatin is completely dissolved, slowly add the bubble bath or soap and a few drops of food coloring. Stir gently to blend (do not beat the mixture because it may become foamy). Pour the mixture in a jar with a lid. Drop in a small toy or some pretty seashells. Put the jar in the refrigerator to set.

To use, place a small amount of jelly under tap water for a bubble bath, or use it as a shower gel.

Corner Bookmarks

When Mom calls you for dinner and it's time to stop reading, use this clever bookmark to hold your place.

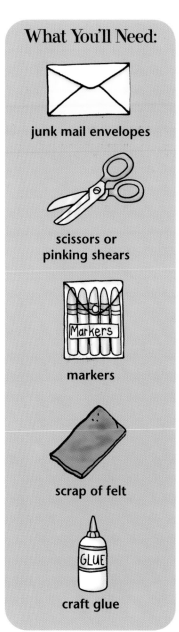

What You'll Need:

junk mail envelopes

scissors or pinking shears

markers

scrap of felt

craft glue

Cut the corners off of your family's junk mail envelopes. (Be sure to ask an adult to show you which envelopes you can use.) For a straight edge, use scissors to cut the corners; if you want a zigzag edge, use pinking shears. Decorate each corner triangle with markers. You could make a bookmark mouse by drawing eyes, ears, whiskers, and a nose on the corner. Then cut a little tail from a scrap of felt, and glue it to the back of the bookmark. To make a sea scene on your bookmark, cut a wavy edge on the corner triangle. Then draw waves and a sailboat. Place the triangle bookmark on a page corner to mark your place in your book.

More than 1 million books were set in place for the official dedication of the New York City Public Library on May 23, 1911. Today, the library's collection includes more than 52 million items!

Movie-Time Scrapbook

You become the film critic!

What You'll Need:

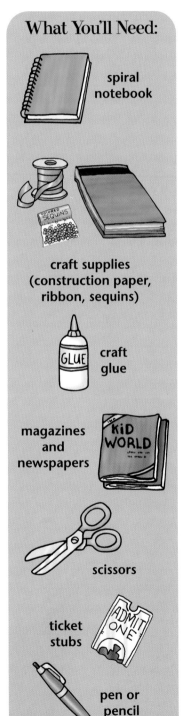

spiral notebook

craft supplies (construction paper, ribbon, sequins)

GLUE craft glue

magazines and newspapers

scissors

ticket stubs

pen or pencil

Are you a film buff? Does going to the latest movie totally rev your jets? Then this fun project is custom-made for you. Keep a movie scrapbook!

Using craft supplies, decorate the cover of a spiral notebook any way you'd like—be creative. Dedicate each page of the notebook to a movie you want to see. Headed for the latest Leonardo DiCaprio flick? Look in magazines and newspapers for print advertisements or reviews of that film. Cut them out, and glue them to a page. Once you actually see the film, date the page, glue on your ticket stub, and take a minute to jot down whether or not the movie was all you'd hoped it would be.

Years from now you'll look back on the scrapbook as a sign of the times. When you're older, you can see how your taste in movies has changed—or stayed the same!

Stick Picture Frames

In the early days of the United States, picture frames might have looked like these. But yours will probably smell better!

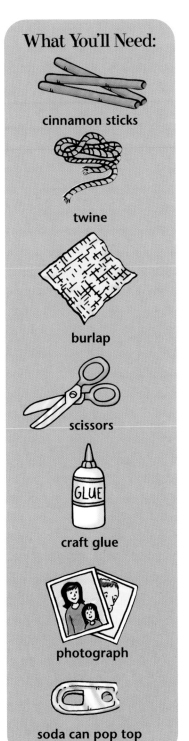

What You'll Need:

cinnamon sticks

twine

burlap

scissors

craft glue

photograph

soda can pop top

Tie 4 cinnamon sticks together at the corners with twine. To make the background, cut out a piece of burlap to fit the size of the frame. Glue the edges of the backing to the back of the cinnamon sticks. Carefully cut your photograph to fit inside the frame; you can make it smaller than the inside of the frame. Center and glue the picture inside the frame. If you want to hang your Stick Picture Frame, glue a metal soda can pop top or a picture hanger to the back.

Paper Doll Chain

*Even though these paper dolls have identical shapes,
you can color each one to look different.*

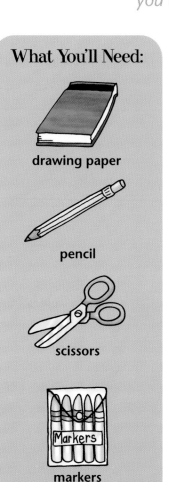

What You'll Need:

drawing paper

pencil

scissors

markers

trims (ribbon, yarn, fabric scraps)

craft glue

Fanfold a piece of drawing paper evenly. To start the fanfold, fold 1 end of the paper over about 1 inch. Then turn the paper over and fold the end up. Continue folding the paper in accordionlike pleats.

After you've finished folding, draw your design for the paper dolls. Make sure at least some parts of the design touch both sides of the paper so the dolls "hold hands." Draw only one half of the doll, since the other half will be across the top fold. Cut out the doll pattern. Then decorate each doll with markers, or glue on trims such as ribbon, yarn, or fabric scraps. You can also make holiday decorations with paper chains of hearts, shamrocks, bunnies, or stars—just remember to leave a part touching each edge.

Paper dolls have been around for more than 100 years. They became very popular in the 1940s when dolls of the day's movie stars were available, such as Lana Turner, Betty Grable, and Judy Garland.

Flower Making Fun

Every vase needs flowers! And these colorful beauties will be perfect for your Stained-Glass Vase (see page 47).

What You'll Need:

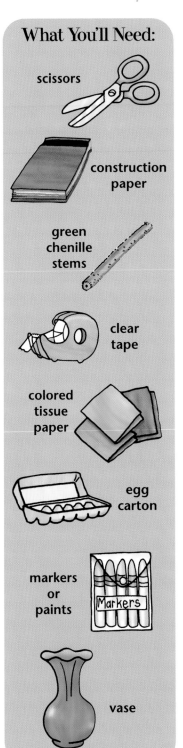

scissors

construction paper

green chenille stems

clear tape

colored tissue paper

egg carton

markers or paints

vase

To make a lily, cut an ice cream cone shape from a piece of construction paper. Overlap the sides of paper together around a chenille stem. Tape the sides to hold it in place. Bend the top end of the chenille stem in a small loop to form the stamen.

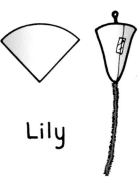

Lily

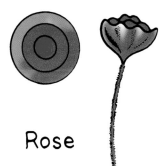

Rose

To make a rose, cut 3 different-size circles from tissue paper. Place the circles on top of each other, and poke a hole in the center. Insert the chenille stem through the center, and twist the bottom of the circles. Secure it with a piece of tape.

To make a tulip, cut 1 cup from an empty egg carton. Trim the edges in the shape of a tulip, and color or paint it your favorite color. Poke a small hole in the center of the cup, and insert a chenille stem.

Tulip

Daffodil

For a daffodil, make a tulip, and add a circle of tissue paper around the bottom of the cup.

Once you have made your flowers, arrange them in a vase, and place the vase in your bedroom or on the kitchen table. To add fragrance to your bouquet, ask an adult for some potpourri to put inside the vase.

Cut a Castle

You'll be the ruler of the land in your very own castle.
Make the Clothespin People on page 117 into your royal subjects.

What You'll Need:

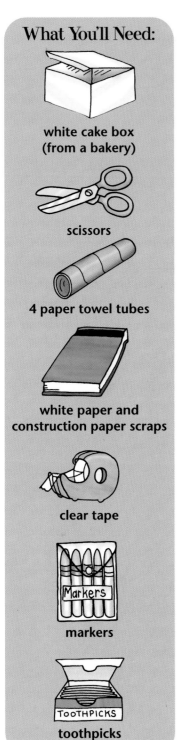

white cake box
(from a bakery)

scissors

4 paper towel tubes

white paper and
construction paper scraps

clear tape

markers

toothpicks

Start this cool project by cutting a drawbridge in the side of the cake box. Then cut out a square from the top of the box—the hole will be the opening for the courtyard, and the rim will be the base for the battlement.

Next, make 4 towers from the paper towel tubes. Wrap white paper around each tube, and secure them with tape. Make a cone for the roof of one of the towers by first cutting a circle out of paper. Then cut a pie-shape wedge from the circle, and wrap and tape the circle to make a cone. Tape the cone to the top of a tube. Then tape a tower to each corner of the box.

To make the wall around the battlement, cut 4 strips of white paper into a comb shape. Make them long enough for each side of the box. Tape the paper around the castle's top edge. Use markers to decorate the castle with windows, vines, and bricks. To make a flag for the castle tower, cut a scrap piece of construction paper in a triangle. Tape it to a toothpick. Insert the toothpick in the top of the cone on the tower, and tape it in place.

Owner Sticks

The Crow Indians used sticks like these to identify the belongings of tribal members. Make some of your own to mark your territory!

What You'll Need:

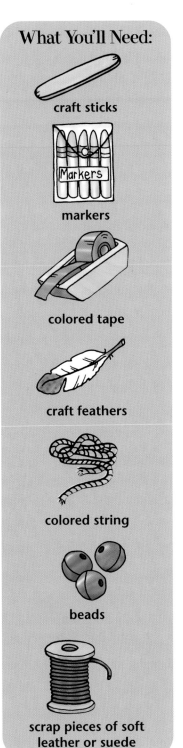

craft sticks

markers

colored tape

craft feathers

colored string

beads

scrap pieces of soft leather or suede

 Instead of using name tags to identify your belongings, use colorful "Owner Sticks," as the Crow Indians of Montana did. Sometimes these sticks were driven into the ground to mark outdoor piles of firewood or deer hides. The sticks were usually about 2 feet long, but you can make smaller versions using wooden craft sticks to keep on your desk or in your backpack.

To make your Owner Stick, draw symbols on a craft stick that best show what you are like, such as a lion if you're brave or a flower if you think you are sweet. Draw lots of different symbols on 1 stick. You can also tape on craft feathers and strings of beads. Wind soft pieces of leather or suede around your sticks. Then make a cross by taping 2 sticks together with colored tape. Decorate your Owner Stick however you like, but make sure that it really shows how unique you are. You may want to make up a Native American name, such as Little Running Deer, and sign it on your stick. If you go camping, drive your Owner Stick in the ground next to your tent to let everyone know you're there!

Military Dog Tags

These dog tags aren't for dogs! They're ID tags like the metal ones American soldiers wear. Cool!

What You'll Need:

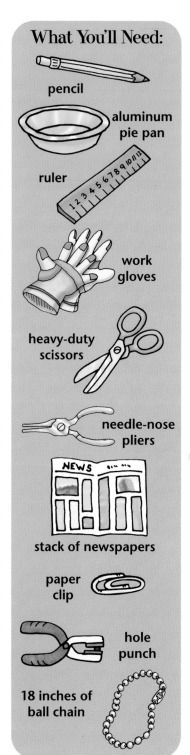

- pencil
- aluminum pie pan
- ruler
- work gloves
- heavy-duty scissors
- needle-nose pliers
- stack of newspapers
- paper clip
- hole punch
- 18 inches of ball chain

Use a pencil to mark two 1½×2¼-inch rectangles on the flat portion of a pie tin. Wearing work gloves, cut out the rectangles with scissors. Trim the corners of the tags diagonally to make a pair of octagons.

Have an adult use the pliers to bend back the edges of the tags about ⅛ inch. Fold the corners first, then the tops and bottoms, and then the sides. Again, wearing your work gloves, place each tag on a hard surface, and use the ruler to gently smooth the edges of the tags by rubbing the ruler along all the folded-down edges. (Have an adult check to make sure there are no sharp edges remaining.)

Now it's time to emboss your initials on the tags with the end of a paper clip. Place the tags on a soft surface, such as a stack of newspapers, and use just enough pressure to raise the letters without poking through the aluminum. Punch a hole in each tag ¼ inch from the top. String your tags, back sides together, onto the ball chain. Then wear your tags with pride!

Millions of American soldiers wear metal identification tags, but only a select few have worn the Medal of Honor. Since the medal's creation in 1861, only 3,400 men and women have received this top award for heroic action in our nation's battles.

Shadow Box

A shadow box (or diorama) is a type of sculpture in which a miniature scene is created that looks like a place you've seen in real life.

What You'll Need:

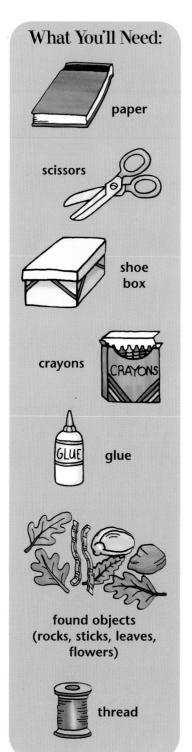

paper

scissors

shoe box

crayons

glue

found objects (rocks, sticks, leaves, flowers)

thread

To make your own diorama, start by cutting a piece of paper to fit on the bottom inside panel of an old shoe box. Then color a background scene on the paper. For example, if you are making a forest scene, you could draw trees and a waterfall on the paper. If you are making an underwater scene, you could color fish, coral, and water on the paper. When your background design is finished, glue the paper to the bottom inside panel of your box.

Now start gluing things to the inside of the box. You can even hang things from the "ceiling" by using thread. Let's say you're creating a beach shadow box. Along the bottom you could spread some glue and then sprinkle sand on it. A small rock could be a boulder. A few twigs with some red crepe paper could be a campfire. A stick could be a log, and a marble could be a beach ball. Get the idea? Have fun!

Beaded Beauties

Make your own beautiful sand beads to wear,
just like the ones worn by African women.

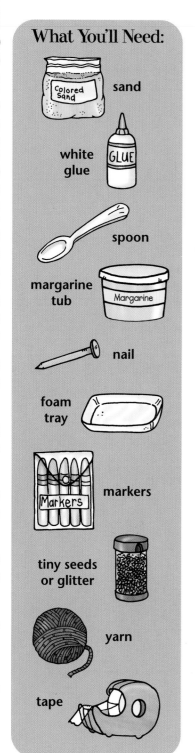

What You'll Need:

sand

white glue

spoon

margarine tub

nail

foam tray

markers

tiny seeds or glitter

yarn

tape

  Mix sand and glue in an empty, clean margarine tub to make sand dough. Make enough dough to roll several beads the size you want. With a nail, poke a hole through the center of the bead. If the dough is too soft to make a hole, add more sand until it is stiff enough to make a hole through the bead. Make lots of beads, then let them dry on a foam tray until they are hard.

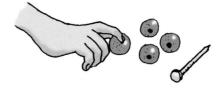

When they are dry, decorate the beads by coloring them with markers or by gluing tiny seeds or bits of glitter to them. To make a necklace, tape 1 end of a piece of yarn (long enough to fit around your neck) to a table, and string the beads onto the yarn. Tie the 2 ends of the yarn together when you've strung all your beads.

You've made beautiful bead jewelry!

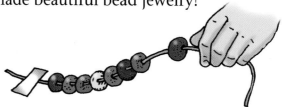

Switchplate Covers

Switch on some fun with this stylish room accent!

What You'll Need:

plastic juice or bleach bottle (washed and rinsed well)

scissors

pencil

paints and paintbrush

craft supplies (sequins, glitter, rhinestones)

COLORED SEQUINS

Markers

markers

GLUE

craft glue

double-sided tape

Tired of seeing that dull old switchplate every time you flip your lights on and off? Why not make a new design that shines with your own ideas?

Cut a piece of plastic from an empty, clean bleach or juice bottle. Ask an adult to unscrew the faceplate in your room so you can use it as a pattern. Place the faceplate on the plastic, trace around it, and cut out the rectangle. Be sure to mark and cut out the center rectangle to make room for the switch. Have an adult replace the faceplate.

Decorate the plastic any way you want. Add sequins or rhinestones if you're in a glamorous mood. Draw tiger stripes if you're feeling wild. Doodle hearts and flowers if you're feeling full of love. Or make the switchplate galactic with stars and asteroids if you're an out-of-this-world kid.

When you're done decorating it, attach your new and improved switchplate over the old one with double-sided tape. (The old switchplate must be in place to keep you safe from electricity.)

Snow Mobile

Bring a little winter inside the house with a sparkling, snowy mobile.

What You'll Need:

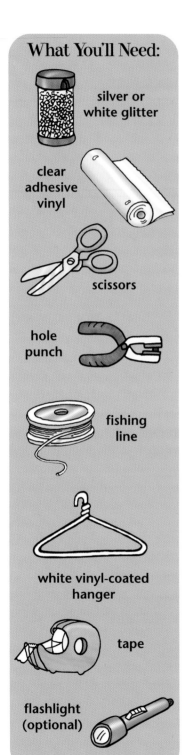

silver or white glitter

clear adhesive vinyl

scissors

hole punch

fishing line

white vinyl-coated hanger

tape

flashlight (optional)

1. Spread silver or white glitter onto the sticky side of a piece of clear adhesive vinyl.

2. Smooth another piece of vinyl over the top, and press out the air bubbles.

3. Cut the glittered adhesive paper into snowballs, snow-people, and snowflakes.

4. Punch a hole near the top of each shape, and thread different lengths of fishing line through each. Your shapes will look like they are floating mysteriously in the air!

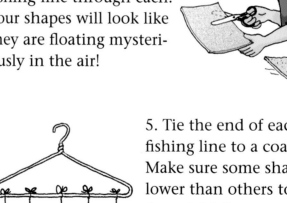

5. Tie the end of each piece of fishing line to a coat hanger. Make sure some shapes hang lower than others to make your Snow Mobile more interesting. To hold the shapes firmly in place, tape the tied ends of the thread to the hanger. Hang your mobile in a dark room, and shine a flashlight for some sparkling fun.

Craft Stick Stick-ins

Dress up plant life with colorful craft-stick fun.

What You'll Need:

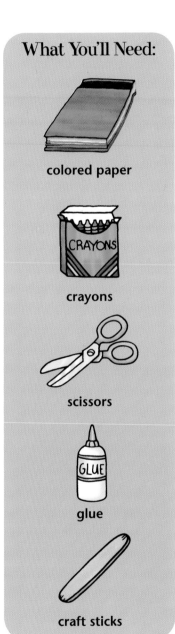

colored paper

crayons

scissors

glue

craft sticks

These adorable stick-ins can spruce up house-plants to make a real cheer-up treat. On colored paper, draw and cut out a butterfly, a ladybug, a bird, or any other design you like. Decorate your designs so they are really special. Then glue your paper design to the end of a craft stick or a clean ice cream stick. Use the other end of the stick to anchor the paper design in the potting soil. Share these cheerful stick-ins with people who might not be able to get out and enjoy the great outdoors.

There are close to 300,000 species of plants that scientists have already named. These plants include mosses that grow close to the ground and huge trees that tower hundreds of feet high. There are plants growing in almost every part of the world today—even in the most difficult climates.

Chapter 3

Games to Play

Spool-a-Word

Spin the spools to make real or pretend words. Even better, spin letters with your friends to invent new word games!

What You'll Need:

3 empty wood spools

unsharpened pencil

markers

Find 3 spools and 1 unsharpened pencil. Using a blue marker, write the letters S, R, L, G, and F around the first spool. Around the second spool, write the letters A, E, I, O, and U in red. Then write the letters N, T, D, P, and B in blue around the third spool. Put the spools on a pencil (in order), and turn them to form a word. Make other spools with more letters, and pick spools with your friends. Put them on a pencil, and see who can come up with the most words in 1 minute.

Ever wonder what the longest word in the English language is? Well, it is 45 letters long and is a type of lung disease. It's pneumonoultramicroscopicsilicovolcanoconiosis. This word is so long there are other big words within it. Can you find them?

Auto Bingo

The next time you take a long car trip, play Auto Bingo.
It will make the time fly by!

What You'll Need:

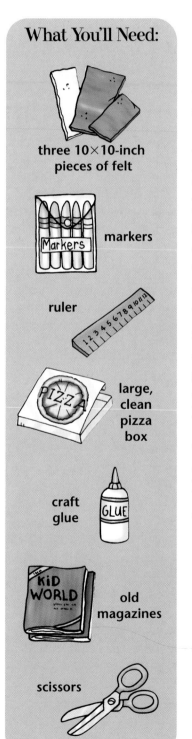

three 10×10-inch
pieces of felt

markers

ruler

large,
clean
pizza
box

craft
glue

old
magazines

scissors

 Use a marker to draw a checkerboard on 2 pieces of felt. To do this, divide each piece into 25 squares, drawing lines 2 inches apart down and across. You should end up with 5 squares down each side. On 1 checkerboard, write "free" in the middle space. Glue this felt piece inside the pizza box on 1 side and the unmarked third felt piece on the other side.

Look through old magazines for pictures of objects you see when you travel—a mail box, speed limit sign, police car, and so on (you will need 24 pictures). Make sure the objects are small enough to fit in a 2-inch square. Cut the objects out. Then, using the other felt piece with a checkerboard, glue each picture onto a 2-inch square. (If you can't find the pictures you need, just draw the objects on the squares.) Cut out the picture squares, and arrange them on the checkerboard felt piece pasted in the box. Fill in all the squares except for the "free" space.

To play, look for the objects on your bingo card when you are taking a car trip. If you see an object, remove the picture square from your card. When you have an empty row across, down, or diagonally, you win!

Balloon Badminton

Your parents always said not to play ball in the house—
until they learned this fun indoor game!

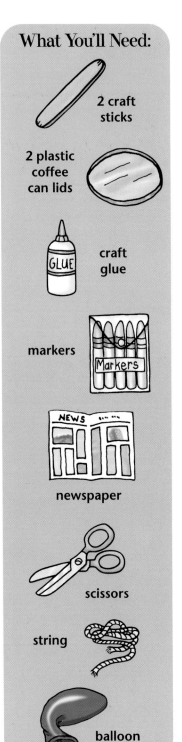

What You'll Need:

2 craft
sticks

2 plastic
coffee
can lids

craft
glue

markers

newspaper

scissors

string

balloon

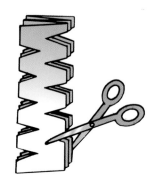

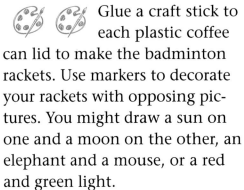 Glue a craft stick to each plastic coffee can lid to make the badminton rackets. Use markers to decorate your rackets with opposing pictures. You might draw a sun on one and a moon on the other, an elephant and a mouse, or a red and green light.

To make the net, fanfold a sheet of newspaper (see Paper Doll Chain on page 52 for help with fanfolding). Then cut out V-sections as shown in the illustration above. Open the paper, and thread some string through the top row of the cutouts. Tie the net to 2 chairs. Blow up a balloon, and play a slow-motion, fun game of badminton inside the house. If you want, decorate the balloon to match your rackets. You might draw a star, a peanut, or a yellow light.

Code Wheel

You and a friend can pretend you're secret agents and send each other important messages in code.

What You'll Need:

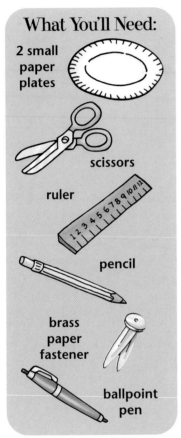

2 small paper plates

scissors

ruler

pencil

brass paper fastener

ballpoint pen

Find 2 small paper plates, or cut out two 6-inch circles from poster board. Cut a ½-inch-wide V-shape and a ½-inch-round window in 1 small paper plate, as shown. Use a pencil to poke a small hole in the center of both plates. Then attach the plates with a brass paper fastener to create your code wheel. Write the letter A in the V, then turn the wheel ½ inch and write the letter B. Continue with the rest of the alphabet around the wheel. (Hint: You can measure ½ inch without a ruler: Make a small pencil mark on the right side of the V, then turn the wheel so the left side lines up with the mark.)

Now fill in the window. Turn the wheel, and write the letter A in the window. (Make sure the V is not pointing to the letter A!) Turn the wheel several inches, and write a B in the window. Write the rest of the alphabet in the window, always making sure the window letter is different than the V letter. Make a second wheel for your friend that matches yours exactly so you can write and decode secret messages.

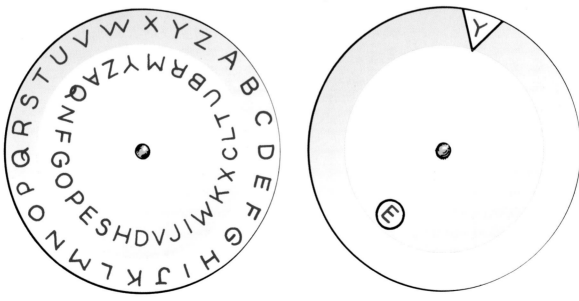

Queen of Stolen Hearts Game

Be quick and outsmart the Queen—steal her hearts!

What You'll Need:

construction paper

scissors

clear tape

fake jewels

glitter

cardboard tube

aluminum foil

ribbons

Make a queen's crown out of a band of construction paper that has been taped together at the ends. Cut out triangular shapes around the band to make the crown's points. Glue on fake jewels and glitter.

Cover a cardboard tube with construction paper. Then form a ball out of foil, and tape it onto the top of the tube to make the queen's scepter. Tape on ribbons to the other end. Decorate a chair with ribbons and more foil to make a throne. Cut out large hearts from red construction paper.

Now you are ready to play the Queen of Stolen Hearts Game. The large hearts are the bases. One person is chosen to be the Queen and sit on the throne. The other players are the Knaves, and they stand on the heart bases. Whoever is left without a heart is the Court Fool. She or he must try to steal a heart whenever the Queen raises her scepter and says, "All change hearts." Whoever is left without a heart to stand on must be the new Court Fool. Players can take turns being the Queen. For variety, the Queen can turn on a tape, a CD, or the radio when she wants the Knaves to change places; players must grab a heart when she turns the music off.

Ring Toss

This is a great game to play at birthday parties.
And you can tell everyone you made it yourself!

What You'll Need:

- 3 toilet paper tubes
- one 12-inch-square piece of cardboard
- masking tape
- construction paper
- scissors
- permanent markers
- 3 plastic coffee can lids

To make the ring toss base, tape each toilet paper tube to the 12-inch piece of cardboard as shown in the illustration. Cut out 3 circles from a piece of construction paper. Then cut a hole out of the center of each circle large enough to fit a toilet paper tube through. Draw point values on each circle: Designate 1 tube as 25 points, another tube as 50 points, and the third as 100 points. Place each circle over a tube, covering the masking tape. Then cut out the center of 3 coffee can lids to make the rings. Decorate each ring with permanent markers.

To play, place the ring toss base flat on the floor, and throw the rings over the tubes. Whoever gets the most points, wins! You may want to stand close to the base when you first start to play. Once you get the hang of it, however, challenge yourself by moving further and further away from the base.

Terrific Trading Cards

*Make your **own** trading cards to swap with your friends.*

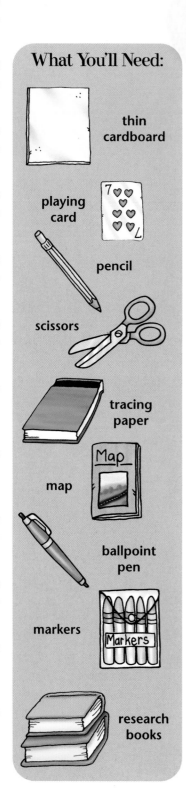

What You'll Need:

thin cardboard

playing card

pencil

scissors

tracing paper

map

ballpoint pen

markers

research books

The United Nations is the peacekeeper for the world. This organization believes that only through international cooperation can humans live together in peace. Trading is one way in which people cooperate. You can make these fun, colorful cards and trade them with your friends.

Lay a playing card on cardboard. Trace around the card, and cut it out. Repeat this for as many trading cards as you want to make. Then trace the outline of a country by placing tracing paper over a map. Transfer the outline by placing the tracing paper on a cardboard cutout and pressing down hard with a pen. Remove the tracing paper, and use a marker to go over the indentations you made with the pen on the cardboard. Write the name of the country inside the outline. Color the card with markers. On the back of the card, draw pictures that show something found in that country, such as official trees and birds or special foods that are prepared there (use research books or the Internet to help you find this information). Write interesting facts about this place under your pictures. Trade these cards with your friends, and collect the world!

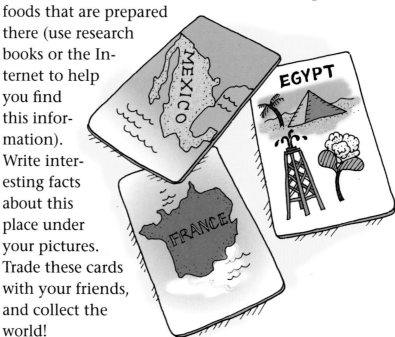

The "Game" Game

*If you find other board games boring,
make your own with these simple directions!*

What You'll Need:

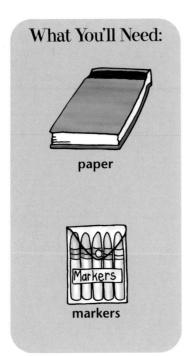

paper

markers

When you draw your own board game, you get to make up all the rules. And the coolest thing about it is you can make one anywhere—all you need is a sheet of paper and some markers.

To get you started, we've given you 2 patterns and some directions that you might want to put on the different squares. You can make the game path like a winding sidewalk, like a coil that spirals around as you move, or like some other shape. You can also put in "shortcuts" so that if a player lands on a certain square, he or she can cut over to a different part of the game.

Try putting some silly directions in the boxes, too, like "Howl like a wolf" or "Put your thumbs in your ears." And whenever you get bored with your board game, remember: You can always make another!

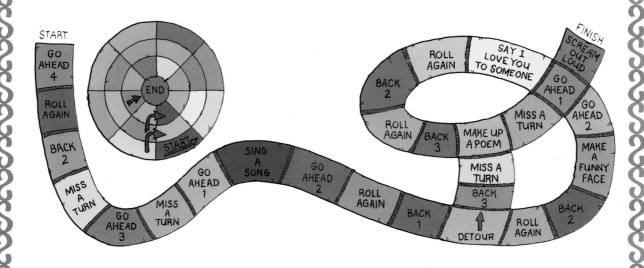

Tic-Tac-Toads

Get hopping on this great new game of 3 in a row!

What You'll Need:

construction paper

crayons

scissors

envelope

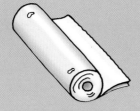

clear adhesive vinyl
(optional)

Give Tic-Tac-Toe a hoppy new boost by using color-coded frogs instead of the traditional X's and O's. Draw and cut out 2 sets of 9 paper frogs. Cut out 1 set from green paper and the other from blue paper (or any color you like best). Draw a standard Tic-Tac-Toe game board as shown in the illustration. Find a friend, and play Tic-Tac-Toads! Be sure to put your leaping game pieces and board in an envelope for safekeeping between games. To make your game extra sturdy, cover the frog game pieces and playing board with clear adhesive vinyl.

Yut-nori

This game has been popular in Korea for more than 1,000 years.

What You'll Need:

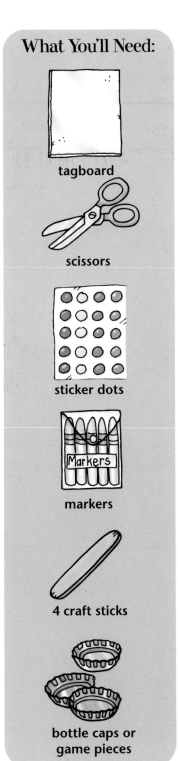

tagboard

scissors

sticker dots

markers

4 craft sticks

bottle caps or game pieces

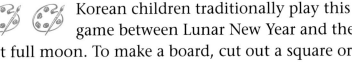 Korean children traditionally play this game between Lunar New Year and the first full moon. To make a board, cut out a square or circle from tagboard. Place the sticker dots in a border around the outside of the square or circle. Designate 1 dot as the starting place by using a different-colored or different-shaped sticker or by coloring around that dot with markers. Then decorate the 4 craft sticks on 1 side only.

To play the game, each player takes a turn tossing the sticks in the air. The player then moves a game piece according to how the sticks land. If all 4 sticks land with the decorated side up, the player moves 4 dots. If 3 sticks land with decorations up, the player moves 3 dots; 2 decorated sticks = 2 dots; 1 decorated stick = 1 dot. And if all the sticks land blank side up, the player moves 5 dots! If a player lands on a dot where another player's game piece is resting, the second player must go back to the starting dot. The first player to make it all the way around the board is the winner!

Make a Tangram

A tangram is like a recyclable puzzle, because you can make so many shapes and patterns with it.

What You'll Need:

one 8×8-inch sheet of thin cardboard

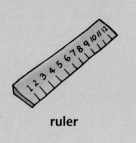

ruler

pencil

crayons or markers

scissors

 Look closely at the pattern in the picture below. Use your ruler and pencil to draw the same pattern onto your sheet of thin cardboard. You can decorate your tangram in many different ways—color each piece a different color, create different patterns on each one, or whatever you like. Then use scissors to cut out the pieces. Note: It is easier to color or decorate your tangram puzzle before you cut it out.

Use the shapes in your tangram kit to make the shapes below. What other shapes can you invent? Draw your tangram shapes, and give them to someone else to try to solve.

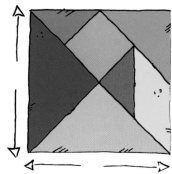

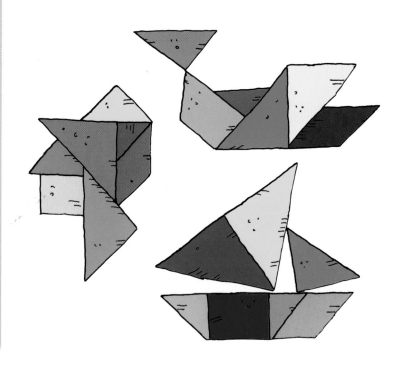

Game Board Book

With this do-it-yourself book, you can take your favorite board games along when you travel—and they'll take up less space than a notebook!

What You'll Need:

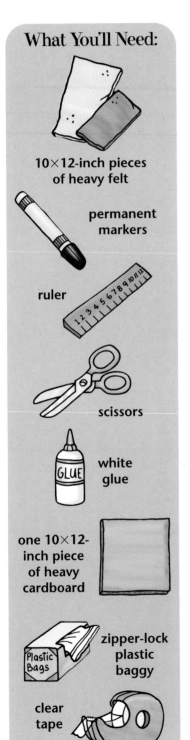

10×12-inch pieces of heavy felt

permanent markers

ruler

scissors

white glue

one 10×12-inch piece of heavy cardboard

zipper-lock plastic baggy

clear tape

Use markers to copy the designs of your favorite game boards onto the pieces of heavy felt. Leave a 1-inch strip of blank space on the left side of each board so you can join them together as a book. Then cut out enough felt pieces so you can play each game you choose to make. Here are just a couple of fun game boards you can make:

Checkers and Chess: Create a game board with 8 rows of 8 squares, and make different playing pieces. To play Checkers, which requires 24 pieces (12 for each player), you can use red and black pieces or any 2 colors you'd like. Chess needs its own special pieces: 16 for each player, 2 colors. Write the name of each piece on 1 side, or draw a picture to show which piece is which.

Tic-Tac-Toe: This board is easy to make, and you can use the Checkers game pieces to play it.

After all your boards are finished, glue them together along the left side like the pages of a book. Then turn the whole thing over, and glue cardboard to the back of the last board. This makes the book stiff enough to play on. You can add new boards at any time by gluing them to the top of the stack. Finally, tape the zipper-lock baggy to the cardboard. Use it to store the felt pieces you make for each game.

Pictominoes

Custom make your dominoes with pictures instead of dots.

What You'll Need:

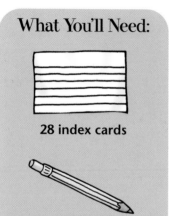

28 index cards

pencil

ink pads

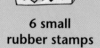

6 small
rubber stamps

On the blank side of each index card, draw a line through the middle from 1 long side to the other. Using one of the ink stamps, make prints on 1 side of 4 index cards. Do the same with the rest of the ink stamps. This should leave you with 4 random spaces that are blank. That's OK; these are wild spaces. Play with your Pictominoes as if they had dots, only match up the pictures instead!

Dominoes are small tiles traditionally carved from ivory or bone. They have been used to play different fun games for many years. In fact, the oldest domino sets date back to 1120 A.D.!

Giant Maze

Create a maze, and challenge your friends to get through it!

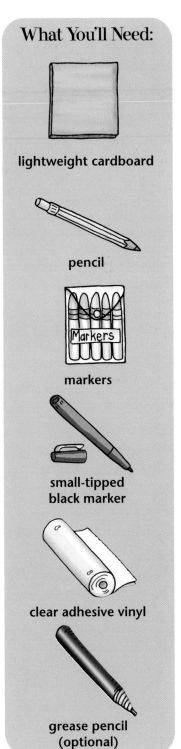

What You'll Need:

lightweight cardboard

pencil

markers

small-tipped black marker

clear adhesive vinyl

grease pencil (optional)

 Use a pencil to draw a maze on a large piece of cardboard. To do this, first draw the correct route through the maze (all the way to the exit). Then make other routes through the maze that look like they lead to the exit but only lead to dead ends. You might want to get ideas from mazes in coloring or activity books.

Why not pick a theme for your maze, with traps and decorated dead ends? Use the markers to illustrate your theme. Is Roger running from a vampire? Is Sara searching for her lollipop? After you've finished drawing and decorating the maze, go back over all the pencil lines with a small-tipped marker.

Cover the board with clear adhesive vinyl so your friends can try escaping from your maze again and again. (Have them use their fingers or a grease pencil, which can be wiped off.)

The Great Adventure

Bring your favorite action hero or heroine to life.

What You'll Need:

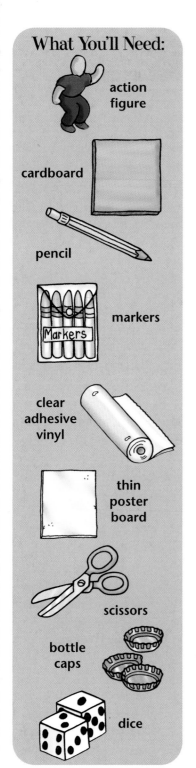

action figure

cardboard

pencil

markers

clear adhesive vinyl

thin poster board

scissors

bottle caps

dice

Come up with an adventure for your favorite hero or heroine action figure. Give him or her a goal to reach and several funny obstacles along the way. Sketch in the starting point in a corner of the cardboard and the end in the opposite corner. Draw a path, with marked spaces big enough for your game pieces, between the starting point and the end. Draw scattered obstacles in the middle, and mark some spaces as "hazard." Finish coloring in the board with markers, then cover it with clear adhesive vinyl for protection. Use the thin poster board to make hazard cards to turn over when you land on one of these spaces. Name the hazard and the penalty, such as "Lose a turn," "Go back 2 spaces," or "Start over." Using bottle caps as game pieces, roll the dice, and begin your adventure!

Crossed Words

*You can make your own crossword puzzle for two
by playing this word-linking game.*

What You'll Need:

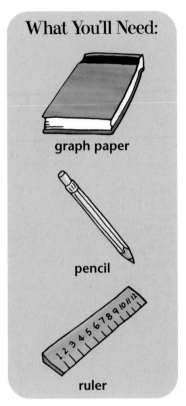

graph paper

pencil

ruler

Mark off a square on your paper that contains 15 boxes down and 15 across. Graph paper works best, but if you don't have any, use a ruler to draw the lines on a piece of blank paper. Outline the box in the very center of the puzzle so that it stands out.

Choose a theme for your puzzle, such as flowers, countries, sports, fruits, vegetables, or another group of objects. Player 1 then needs to think of a word that fits into the chosen category. He or she writes the word on the page, 1 letter per box. The first word must have at least 1 letter that goes through the middle box.

Players take turns thinking of words and writing them down. The tricky part is that every word must share a letter with a word that's already on the page. Score 1 point for each letter in a word—but don't count any letters you "borrow" from another word. Play until nobody can think of any more words that will fit on the graph. The player with the highest score wins!

The first modern crossword puzzle was published on December 21, 1913, in the New York World's Sunday supplement, Fun. This started a "crossword craze," and soon the puzzles were being published in most of the leading U.S. newspapers.

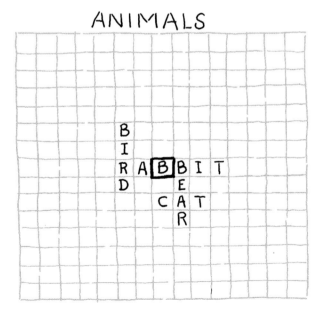

ANIMALS

Portable Soccer Game

Baseball and football aren't the most popular sports in the world—soccer is! Now you can enjoy this game anywhere with this portable, tabletop version.

What You'll Need:

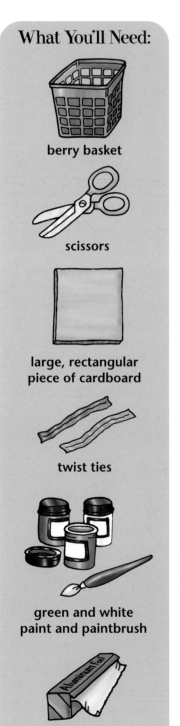

berry basket

scissors

large, rectangular piece of cardboard

twist ties

green and white paint and paintbrush

aluminum foil

Cut a berry basket in half; each half will be a goal. Center 1 berry-basket goal on 1 short end of the cardboard. Starting on the right side of the berry basket, poke 2 holes next to each other in the cardboard—one on the inside of the basket, the other on the outside. Repeat for the left side of the basket. Attach the goal to the cardboard by bending a twist tie through the berry basket and through each pair of holes in the cardboard. Twist tie the ends together underneath the cardboard. Repeat the process for the other short side of the cardboard with the other berry-basket goal.

To make the cardboard look like a soccer field, paint the board using green for grass and white for the boundary lines. Make a ball from foil. Turn your hand into a soccer player—use your pointer and middle fingers as legs to kick the ball. Now it's time to find an opponent and start playing!

Giant Dice

No more lost dice. These oversized cubes are fun to use and hard to lose!

What You'll Need:

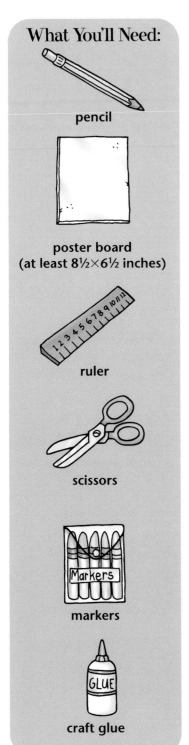

pencil

poster board
(at least 8½×6½ inches)

ruler

scissors

markers

craft glue

Draw the pattern shown below on the poster board. (Make a bigger pattern for larger dice.) Be sure to follow the dimensions exactly. Each square is 2 inches on each side; the tabs are ½ inch wide. Cut along the solid lines, and score on the dotted lines. Scoring makes it easier to fold the poster board. To score, use a ruler to guide the point of your scissors as you "draw a line" along the dotted lines.

Decorate the 6 squares with markers. Make dots as on regular dice, or draw numbers, letters, or shapes. Make the cutout into a box by folding along the scored lines. Place glue on the tabs, and tuck them inside the box to hold it together.

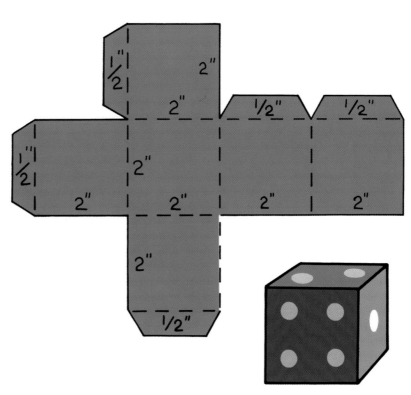

Chapter 4
Celebrations!

New Year's Garland

Make these lacy garlands out of colored paper, and string them up in your home when it's time to celebrate the New Year.

What You'll Need:

construction paper

scissors

ruler

craft glue

Cut twelve 4-inch circles out of different-colored paper. Fold each circle in half, in half again, and, finally, in half a third time. Your circles should now look like slices of pie. Cut out a series of small snips from both folded edges. Unfold the snipped circles.

Apply glue just along the edge of 1 circle. Place a second circle on top of the first so that the edges stick together. Apply glue to the center (not the edge) of the second circle, and place a third circle on top of it. Continue adding the remaining circles, alternately gluing the edges and the centers. When the glue is dry, gently pull the top and bottom circle in opposite directions.

Hang the stretched garland for your New Year's celebration!

Eid ul-Fitr Cards

Experiment with different geometric shapes and patterns to make these cool, colorful cards.

What You'll Need:

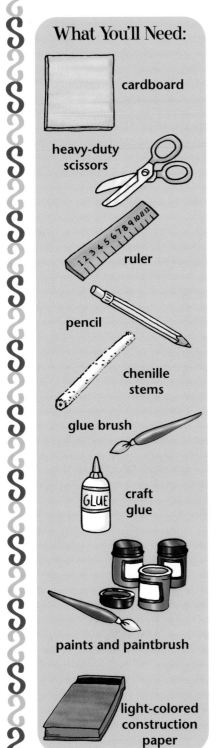

cardboard

heavy-duty scissors

ruler

pencil

chenille stems

glue brush

craft glue

paints and paintbrush

light-colored construction paper

 Eid ul-Fitr is an important Muslim festival, during which people give each other presents and cards. The Muslim religion forbids the drawing of people or animals, so these cards are decorated with designs made from geometric shapes and patterns.

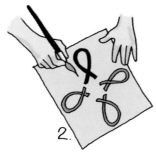 To begin, cut out a 3-inch square of cardboard with the heavy-duty scissors (you may need an adult to help you). On the cardboard square, draw a rough pencil sketch of the geometric pattern you want to print. Twist the chenille stems into the shapes that make up your pattern. Brush a thin layer of glue onto your cardboard pattern. While the glue is wet, press the chenille-stem shapes onto the design. Let the glue dry completely.

Use a paintbrush to apply paint to the raised pattern on your cardboard (this is your printing block). Place the printing block on top of a piece of scrap paper, and gently press down on the block. Carefully pull the block away from the paper to see the printed pattern. Practice printing on the scrap paper a few times before printing your designs on folded sheets of light-colored construction paper to make cards.

Peace Plane

Fly a flock of peaceful doves to celebrate Martin Luther King, Jr., Day.

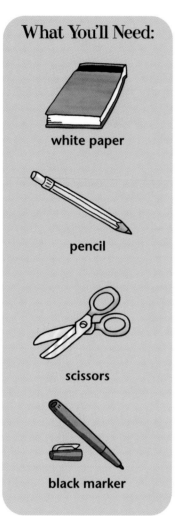

What You'll Need:

white paper

pencil

scissors

black marker

Bring peace into your house—and the sky above it—with these easy-to-make paper doves.

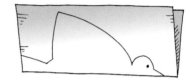

1. Fold an 8½×11-inch piece of white paper in half.

2. Draw the side view of a dove as shown above.

3. Cut off the extra paper around the outline of the dove.

4. Fold each wing down to make an airplane shape.

5. Write a peaceful message or a quote from Dr. Martin Luther King, Jr., such as "I Have a Dream," inside the dove.

6. Let peace fly!

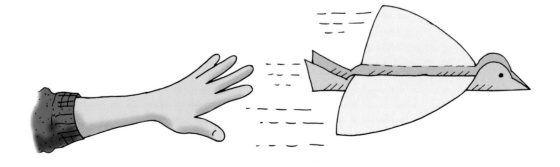

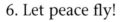

Folded Fireworks

There are always fireworks on Chinese New Year—the Chinese invented fireworks! Now you can make your own fireworks out of tissue paper.

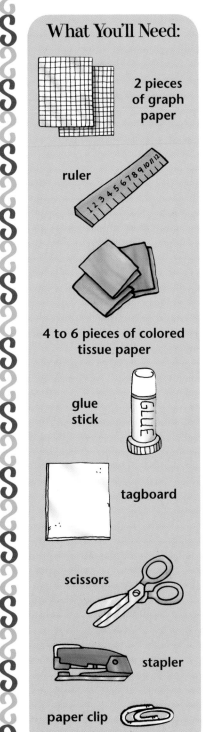

What You'll Need:

2 pieces of graph paper

ruler

4 to 6 pieces of colored tissue paper

glue stick

tagboard

scissors

stapler

paper clip

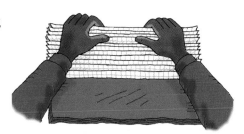

1. Stack 2 pieces of graph paper. Accordion fold them along the lines into ¾-inch folds.

2. Unfold, and place 4 to 6 pieces of tissue paper between the graph paper. Then refold to make fold marks in the tissue paper.

3. Take a piece of folded tissue paper, and put a line of glue on the inside edge of the first fold. Then take the next piece of tissue paper, and place the inside edge of the first fold over the glued edge. Continue in the same way with all the sheets of tissue paper, making 1 long continuous pleated sheet.

4. Cut 2 pieces of tagboard the same length as the connected tissue sheets but half as wide as the folded edge. Completely cover 1 side of each piece of tagboard with glue. Glue 1 piece on top of your stack of tissue paper and the other on the bottom. At the very top edge, staple the pieces of tagboard together (with the tissue paper in between). Let the glue dry.

5. Spread the tissue-paper fireworks until the tagboard sides are back-to-back. Fasten with a paper clip.

Birch Bark Valentines

Make special valentines out of natural treasures and your own words.

What You'll Need:

thin birch bark
(use only fallen or loose
bark that is peeling off
naturally)

natural objects
(flowers, feathers,
evergreen sprigs)

ink pen

ribbon

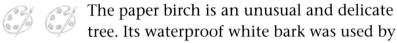 The paper birch is an unusual and delicate tree. Its waterproof white bark was used by Native Americans to make canoes. It can also be used like paper to make these valentines. Find a paper birch tree with thin strips of bark that have fallen or are already peeling off. Tear off only what you will use. Be careful not to tear off living bark—it could harm the tree!

Next, take a walk in a park, a woodland, or another place where you can find early flowers, feathers, or evergreen sprigs. With permission, collect a few natural treasures that you think are pretty. Lay your treasures out at home, and let them inspire a Valentine's Day poem. Evergreen sprigs may make you think of a friendship that is "ever green" (one that will last forever). Flowers may stand for a blossoming friendship.

When you have composed your poem, write it on a piece of birch bark. Roll the bark around the feathers, flowers, or whatever objects you have used in your poem. Tie the valentine with a ribbon, and surprise someone on Valentine's Day—or any day!

Roses are red
Violets are blue
Some poems rhyme
Others don't

Heart Flowers

Give your valentine colorful flowers, even in the middle of winter.

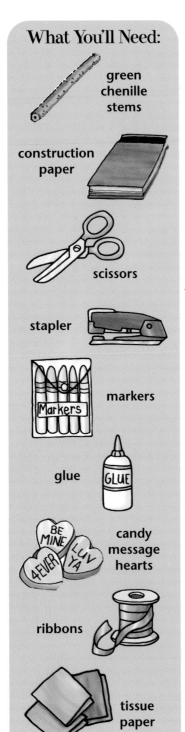

What You'll Need:

green chenille stems

construction paper

scissors

stapler

markers

glue

candy message hearts

ribbons

tissue paper

Take a bouquet of heart-shape flowers to a loved one this Valentine's Day. Use chenille stems to make the stems of your flowers. You may want some flowers to be longer than others to give your bouquet more variety. You can do this by laying 2 chenille stems end to end and twisting the ends together.

Cut 2 same-size hearts out of construction paper. You will need 2 hearts for each flower you want to make. You might want to cut each set of hearts different sizes to add variety to your bouquet. Then staple the hearts front to back around the stem so that the chenille stem is held tightly in place.

Decorate the hearts with markers and by gluing on 1 or 2 tiny candy message hearts. Tie ribbons in bows around the stems, then gather the bunch of heart flowers, and wrap them in tissue paper. Tie the tissue-paper cone with more ribbons to keep the flowers together. Then present your bouquet of heart flowers to your valentine!

Japanese Egg Doll

*Observe the Japanese holiday Hinamatsuri, or Doll's Festival,
by making your own Hina-dolls!*

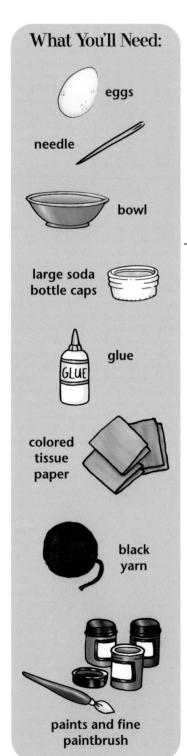

What You'll Need:

eggs

needle

bowl

large soda
bottle caps

glue

colored
tissue
paper

black
yarn

paints and fine
paintbrush

You can make your own Hina-dolls to help you celebrate Hinamatsuri. Use a needle to make a small hole in 1 end of a raw egg. Stick the needle through the hole to break the yolk. Then make a slightly larger hole in the other end of the egg, again using a needle. Hold the egg over a bowl, and blow through the small hole until the raw egg comes out of the larger hole. You have to blow hard! When the eggshell is empty, gently rinse out the inside, and wash the outside. Let the shell dry. Then glue the large end of the egg into a soda bottle cap so that the egg will stand up. Use tissue paper to make kimonos for your doll. Glue on black yarn for hair, and paint the doll's face. Repeat these steps to create more dolls. Then use the raw eggs to bake a cake, and have a Hinamatsuri tea party!

Leprechaun Bubble Pipe

Legend says that fairies catch rides on bubbles made from leprechaun pipes. Here's your chance to find out!

What You'll Need:

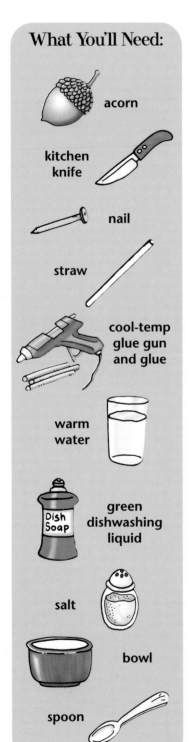

acorn

kitchen knife

nail

straw

cool-temp glue gun and glue

warm water

green dishwashing liquid

salt

bowl

spoon

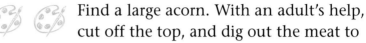 Find a large acorn. With an adult's help, cut off the top, and dig out the meat to make a little bowl. Using a nail, carefully make a hole in the side of the acorn near the bottom of the bowl, just big enough for a straw to fit through. Put the straw into the hole, and fill the area around the straw with glue (ask an adult for help with the glue gun). Blow gently through the straw to make sure no glue is clogging the hole. Then set the bubble pipe aside.

Mix up some bubble solution by combining 1 cup of warm water, ½ cup of green dishwashing liquid, and 1 teaspoon of salt in a bowl. Stir the mixture until the salt dissolves.

Now it's time to give bubble rides to some leprechauns! Dip the pipe in the bubble solution, and blow gently.

Tiny Easter Baskets

These baskets are so easy to make, you'll want to create a whole bunch to use as table decorations and to give to your friends!

What You'll Need:

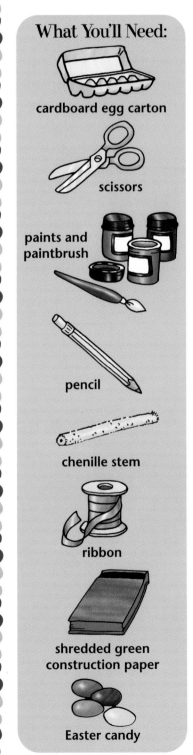

cardboard egg carton

scissors

paints and paintbrush

pencil

chenille stem

ribbon

shredded green construction paper

Easter candy

Separate the individual sections of an egg carton with scissors (you may need an adult to help you). Paint the sections in your favorite colors, and let dry. Next, make handles for the Easter baskets by using a sharp pencil point to poke a hole on 2 opposite sides of an egg carton section. Insert 1 end of a chenille stem in 1 hole, and bend the end of the stem so it will stay in place. Then make an arch over the egg carton section with the chenille stem, and insert the other end in the opposite hole. Again, bend the end of the chenille stem to secure the handle. For an added touch, tie a bow to the top of the handle. Fill the baskets with shredded green construction paper, then add your favorite Easter goodies.

In some countries such as Austria, France, Norway, and Syria, an egg-knocking game is played at Easter. The object is to hit everyone else's egg without breaking your own egg. The last player with a whole egg is the winner!

Beautiful Bonnet

Have you ever wished you could make your own Easter bonnet just the color and shape you wanted? Well, now you can!

What You'll Need:

2 pieces of wrapping paper

white paste

4 sheets of newspaper

heavy-duty scissors

bowl (the size of your head)

decorations (ribbons, flowers, buttons)

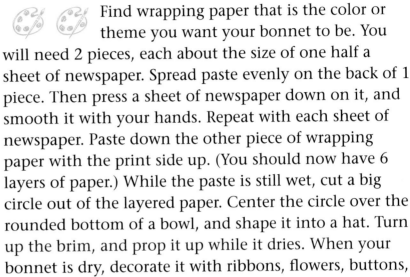 Find wrapping paper that is the color or theme you want your bonnet to be. You will need 2 pieces, each about the size of one half a sheet of newspaper. Spread paste evenly on the back of 1 piece. Then press a sheet of newspaper down on it, and smooth it with your hands. Repeat with each sheet of newspaper. Paste down the other piece of wrapping paper with the print side up. (You should now have 6 layers of paper.) While the paste is still wet, cut a big circle out of the layered paper. Center the circle over the rounded bottom of a bowl, and shape it into a hat. Turn up the brim, and prop it up while it dries. When your bonnet is dry, decorate it with ribbons, flowers, buttons, and bows.

Elijah's Cup

The prophet Elijah will visit your house with joy when he can drink from this lovely goblet.

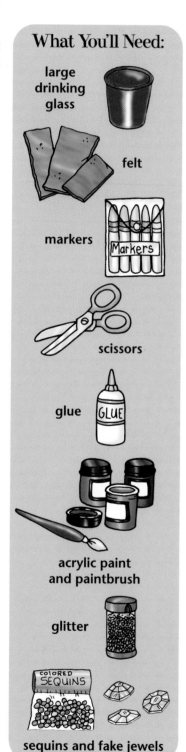

What You'll Need:

large drinking glass

felt

markers

scissors

glue

acrylic paint and paintbrush

glitter

sequins and fake jewels

The prophet Elijah is busy at Passover. Think of all the homes he will visit and how many different wine glasses he will sip from! Show him how pleased you are to welcome him into your house with this specially decorated glass.

Wash and dry a drinking glass or wine glass (plastic may be used for younger children). Place the glass on a piece of felt, and trace around the bottom to make a circle. Cut out the circle, and glue it on the bottom of the glass. Cover your work surface, and paint a design on your glass with acrylic paint. Once the paint is dry, you can write the name "Elijah" in glue as part of your design and sprinkle glitter on it. If you like, glue sequins and fake jewels around the top and bottom of the glass. Make Elijah's cup as fancy as you like. These glasses also make nice presents if you are invited to seder at a friend's or relative's home.

Before Passover, many Jews clean their homes of chametz, which is leavening (it makes breads and cakes rise). A complete cleaning of the house is done, sometimes starting weeks before Passover begins. All leavened foods must be taken out of the house, and all crumbs must be cleaned out completely.

Paper Lotus Chain

Celebrate Buddha's birthday with this beautiful lotus chain.

What You'll Need:

white paper

pencil

scissors

pink and green tissue paper

straight pins

white glue

Use the leaf and petal patterns below as guides to make your own patterns out of white paper. Then make stacks of 5 to 10 pieces of tissue paper. Pin the patterns to the tissue paper, and cut them out. You will need 1 green leaf piece for every 2 pink petal pieces. The more pieces you cut, the longer your garland will be. When all of the petals and leaves are cut, lay a green leaf on the table. Put a dot of glue in the middle of the leaf, and press a petal on top of it. Put a dot of glue on each point of the petal, and press another pink petal on top. Then put a dot of glue in the middle of the top pink petal, and add a green leaf. Repeat this pattern until you have used all the tissue paper. Remember, green leaves are glued to petals in the center; petals are glued to petals at the points. Let the glue dry. When you stretch out your creation, you will have a beautiful lotus garland!

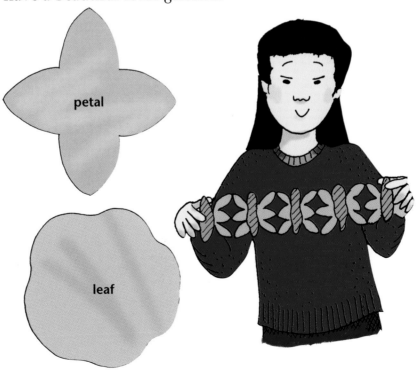

petal

leaf

Garbage Gobbler

Make the planet beautiful and trash-free with help from this energetic Earth Day Garbage Gobbler!

What You'll Need:

large cardboard box

heavy-duty scissors

paint and paintbrush

glue

24 inches of thin rope

work gloves

On Earth Day, people all over the world celebrate the earth's wonderful natural resources. Think of what the planet would be like without green grass, clean oceans, or the lovely smell of fresh flowers. When people neglect to throw their trash in garbage cans, they are destroying this natural beauty. That's where you and your Garbage Gobbler come in to save the day!

Have an adult help you cut the flaps off a cardboard box so that the top is open. This is the Garbage Gobbler's big, empty belly. Paint the box to look like a fantastic creature. Nobody has ever seen a Garbage Gobbler before, so you can make your creature look however you want. An adult can help you cut a nose, a tail, and ears from the extra cardboard. Attach these parts to the Gobbler with glue. When the paint and glue are dry, ask an adult to cut a small hole in the front of the box to attach the rope for the Gobbler's leash. Once you have your Garbage Gobbler ready, walk it around your neighborhood, and start filling up its empty belly with trash. Wear work gloves when you pick up trash, and be very careful of broken glass. Also, don't forget to wash your hands after you're done feeding the Garbage Gobbler!

Magnets de Mayo

These colorful flowers are actually made of corn and beans!

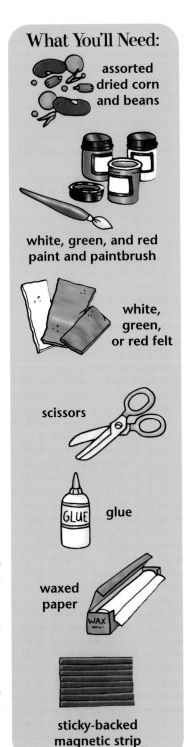

What You'll Need:

- assorted dried corn and beans
- white, green, and red paint and paintbrush
- white, green, or red felt
- scissors
- glue
- waxed paper
- sticky-backed magnetic strip

Green, white, and red are the colors of the Mexican flag. You can combine these colors in lots of interesting ways when painting the corn and beans that make up these flower magnets. Use an assortment of dried beans to vary the shape of your flowers. Tiny lentils and corn kernels will make delicate posies, while larger fava beans can become the leaves of a gorgeous bloom.

Start by painting lots of dried beans and corn in the colors of Mexico, and let dry. Then arrange 6 to 10 beans and kernels in a flower shape. Cut out a circle of felt a bit larger than your flower. Cover the circle with glue, and arrange your flower on it. Put the felt flower on waxed paper, and cover it completely with glue. If some of the glue runs over the edges of your flower, don't worry. You can break off the extra glue when it is dry. When your flower is completely dry, peel it off the waxed paper, and attach a sticky-backed magnetic strip on the back of the felt circle.

Float a Flower Boat

Decorate a homemade toy boat in honor of soldiers who died at sea.

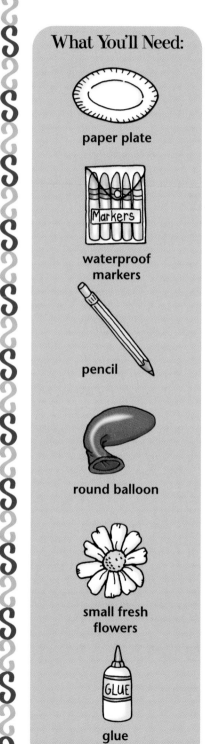

What You'll Need:

paper plate

waterproof markers

pencil

round balloon

small fresh flowers

glue

Every Memorial Day, the navy floats flowers out into the ocean to honor soldiers who died at sea. Take part in this tradition by making a flower boat out of a balloon, a paper plate, and your creativity!

Draw colorful flowers with waterproof markers on a paper plate. Poke a hole in the center of the plate with a pencil. Then put the open end of a round balloon through the hole. Blow up the balloon (from the back of the plate) until it is full. Knot the balloon.

To make your boat extra special, glue small fresh flowers or wildflowers onto the balloon and plate. Make a few different balloon boats, and send them "off to sea" as a beautiful, flowery thank you to the men and women who gave their lives to preserve freedom. You could launch your flower boats in a nearby pond, lake, or other body of water, but be sure to get your parents' permission first! And don't forget to collect the balloons and throw them away when you are done, as balloons can be harmful to wildlife.

Flag Windsock

*You'll feel as free as the breeze when you catch
the wind in this decorative windsock.*

What You'll Need:

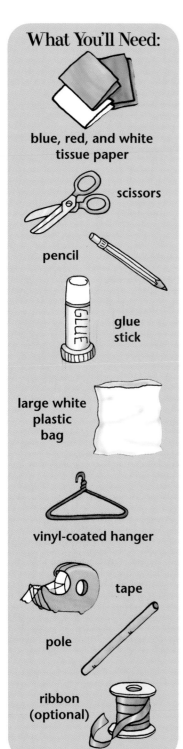

blue, red, and white
tissue paper

scissors

pencil

glue
stick

large white
plastic
bag

vinyl-coated hanger

tape

pole

ribbon
(optional)

  This windsock will be fun to play with at your July 4th picnic. It looks pretty, too!

To make it, cut out a large square of blue tissue paper. Draw and cut out white tissue-paper stars, and glue them to the blue background. Then glue this onto a large white plastic bag. Next, cut out red and white tissue-paper stripes, and glue these to the bag to make the American flag. Make a large hoop from a vinyl-coated hanger or thick wire (have an adult help you with this). Fold about 2 inches of the bag over the hoop, and tape it. Attach the windsock to a pole with loose wire loops so your windsock can change direction in the wind. If you like, tie long red, white, and blue ribbons to the top of the pole to make streamers.

This windsock works best on a breezy day, but if you run with it, the bag will fill with air and float as you create your own wind. (Note: Keep plastic bags away from small children—plastic is a choking hazard!)

Rakhi (Hindu Plaited Bracelet)

These bracelets are given to family members at Raksha Bandhan, a Hindu and Sikh festival. You can give your rakhi to a family member or friend, too!

What You'll Need:

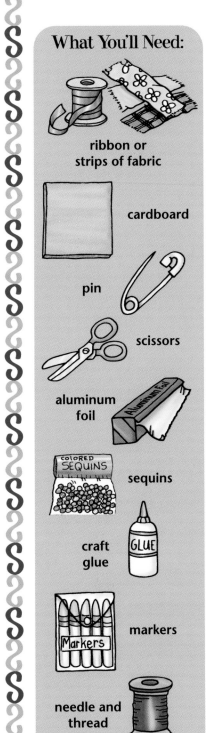

ribbon or strips of fabric

cardboard

pin

scissors

aluminum foil

sequins

craft glue

markers

needle and thread

Use ribbon or strips of fabric that are more than double the length of the bracelet you want. To make a 3-strand rakhi, knot the ends of 3 pieces of ribbon or fabric together. Pin the ribbon or fabric to a piece of heavy cardboard so it is easier to work with. Braid the ribbon or fabric as shown in the diagram. Continue braiding in this manner until you have braided almost all of the length of ribbon or fabric. To finish the braid, knot the ends of the ribbon or fabric together. Cut a small circle out of cardboard, and decorate it with foil, sequins, and markers. Sew the decorated circle to the middle of the plaited band. To wear the plait as a bracelet, tie it around your wrist.

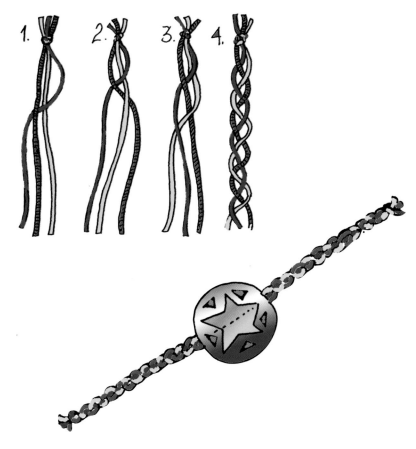

Honey Cards

Your friends and family will think you're as sweet as honey when you send out these New Year's cards!

What You'll Need:

heavyweight paper

pencil

scissors

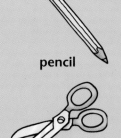

felt

markers

glue

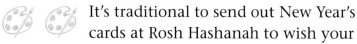 It's traditional to send out New Year's cards at Rosh Hashanah to wish your friends and family a sweet year. To make a honey of a card, draw a large honey jar on a folded piece of heavy-weight paper. The left side of the jar will be along the fold. Cut out the honey jar shape except the folded edge. Trace the jar shape twice on a piece of felt. Cut out the 2 felt jars, and glue them onto the front and back of your card. Cut an oval shape out of felt to use as the honey jar's label. Write the word "HONEY" on it with a marker, and glue it onto the front of the card. Inside the card, draw pictures, and write the message, "May your New Year be as sweet as honey!" Everyone will agree that this is one sweet card!

Pumpkin-Head Twirlers

This pumpkin-head person never tires of going 'round and 'round!

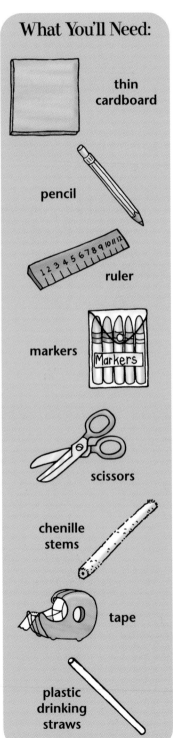

What You'll Need:

thin cardboard

pencil

ruler

markers

scissors

chenille stems

tape

plastic drinking straws

This is an amusing and acrobatic toy. To make it, draw the head and trunk (no arms or legs) of a little person about 4 inches tall on a piece of thin cardboard. Instead of a human head, however, draw a pumpkin with a face on it. Give it a funny hat if you want. Then use markers to decorate it. Cut out the pumpkin-head person, and tape chenille stems to its back to form arms and legs. Use 1 horseshoe-shape piece for both arms, and another horseshoe-shape piece for the legs. Wrap the ends of the arms around a drinking straw so your pumpkin-head person is holding on to the straw like a trapeze artist. When you twirl the ends of the straw, watch the tricks begin! Make another pumpkin-head person, but this time wrap the ends of its legs around the straw. You can create a whole circus of pumpkin-head performers!

Tabletop Gobbler

Make an edible centerpiece for your Thanksgiving table!

What You'll Need:

apple

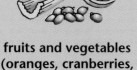

fruits and vegetables
(oranges, cranberries,
celery)

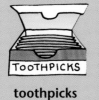

knife

toothpicks

Place an apple on a table with the stem facing down. This is the body of the turkey. Have an adult help you gather and cut up a variety of fruits and vegetables, such as oranges, raisins, peas, cranberries, carrots, and celery. Then start working on your turkey. Use the toothpicks to stick the pieces of fruit and vegetables onto the turkey.

Try making a tail, a head, a beak, eyes, feet, and anything else you can think of. Use your imagination, and don't worry if your turkey doesn't look like the real thing. It will be a wonderful decoration for your Thanksgiving dinner table! And you can eat your turkey for a healthy snack. (Note: Don't eat the cranberries; they are very tart.)

Pilgrim Seed Pictures

It will take patient hands to make this 3-D picture.

What You'll Need:

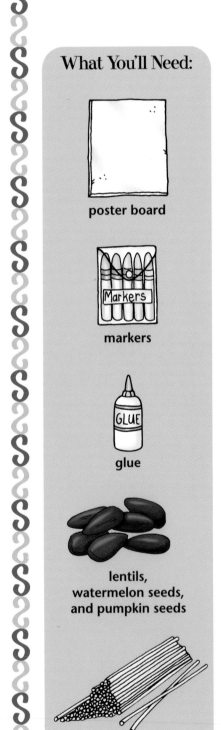

poster board

markers

glue

lentils,
watermelon seeds,
and pumpkin seeds

uncooked
spaghetti

From tiny seeds grow mighty trees—and mighty pilgrims, too! Draw a large outline of a pilgrim on a piece of poster board. Give him a hat, knee breeches, a shirt with a collar or a short jacket, a belt, long stockings, and shoes. Then glue seeds one at a time to fill in the outline. Overlap the seeds to fill in all the gaps. Use watermelon seeds for the black hat, shoes, and belt. You can color pumpkin seeds with markers to fill in other areas. Lentils can be used for the eyes, nose, and mouth. Break pieces of uncooked spaghetti to glue on for the hair. You will have to work carefully to make this picture, but you'll have the patience of a pilgrim when you are through!

The first Thanksgiving feast, celebrated by the Pilgrims in 1621, wasn't even called Thanksgiving at the time. It was almost 250 years later when Sarah Josepha Hale, author of the poem "Mary Had a Little Lamb," convinced President Abraham Lincoln to proclaim Thanksgiving a national holiday.

Hanukkah Spinning Stars

Watch the stars spin on this colorful mobile!

What You'll Need:

8½ × 11-inch
white paper

pencil

scissors

construction
paper

string

tape

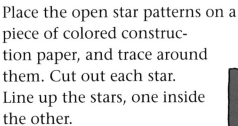
Fold a piece of white paper in half. Draw one half of a large Star of David on the paper, keeping the center of the star on the folded edge. Cut out the star. Unfold the paper, and draw another star inside the larger star. Cut out the smaller star, making sure you keep the Star of David shape.

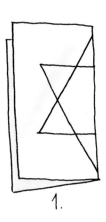

1.

Place the open star patterns on a piece of colored construction paper, and trace around them. Cut out each star. Line up the stars, one inside the other.

2.

Cut a piece of string; the string should be slightly longer than the distance between the inside star and the bigger star. Tape the string in place, but be sure the smaller star moves inside the larger star. Cut another, longer piece of string, and glue or tape the string to the top of the larger star. Make a loop at the end of the top string for hanging.

Hang the mobile away from a wall, then watch the stars spin! (Note: Try shiny wrapping paper for shimmery, shiny stars.)

3.

Star of David Bookmarks

Latkes are not the only use you'll have for potatoes this Hanukkah!

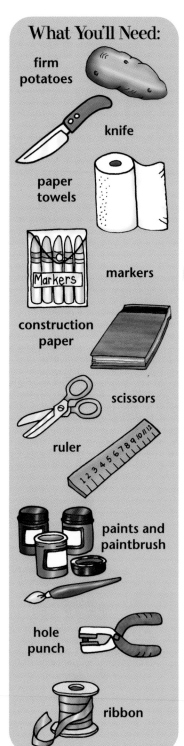

What You'll Need:

- firm potatoes
- knife
- paper towels
- markers
- construction paper
- scissors
- ruler
- paints and paintbrush
- hole punch
- ribbon

Have an adult help you with the cutting in this project. To begin, wash a firm potato, then cut it in half. Pat the potato dry with a paper towel. Using a marker, draw a Star of David on the white part of one of the potato halves. Carefully cut the potato away around the star outline. When you finish you will have a raised star.

Now cut 12-inch-long rectangles from construction paper—cut them a little wider than your potato star shape. Brush a thick, even layer of paint onto the star shape. Carefully press it onto a rectangle, then lift the potato straight up—don't wiggle or drag it. Print a row of stars, or paint half of the star shape 1 color and the other half a different color.

When the paint is dry, write messages on the bookmarks, such as "Happy Hanukkah." Punch a hole in the top of the bookmark, thread a ribbon through the hole, and make a knot.

Animal Anklet

Decorate your ankle with wild beasts!

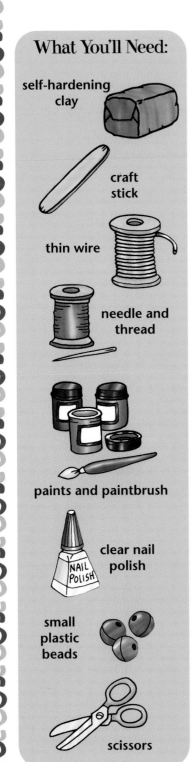

What You'll Need:

self-hardening clay

craft stick

thin wire

needle and thread

paints and paintbrush

clear nail polish

NAIL POLISH

small plastic beads

scissors

Wear some of Africa's special creatures to your next Kwanza party. These animal beads are so small that you can string together a whole herd!

To make your tiny bead animals, roll self-hardening clay into balls the size of grapes. You can make elephants, giraffes, zebras, monkeys, or anything you want! Use a craft stick to help you form legs, ears, horns, and trunks. You can also use small pieces of thin wire to make tails or tusks. After you've made all the animals you'd like, poke a needle through the back of each animal to make a hole. Turn the needle gently to make the hole big enough for thread to pass through. Let the animals dry until the clay is hard.

Now you're ready to paint the animals with bright colors. When the paint is dry, apply a coat of clear nail polish on the animals. Measure a length of thin wire that will fit comfortably around your ankle. Leave a little extra to make a hook and loop to open and close the anklet. String small plastic beads onto the wire. Then thread a needle with colored thread, and knot the end. Thread the needle through a small bead on the anklet and then through one of your clay animals. Thread through a few more beads, then tie the thread onto the anklet so that the animal hangs down. Repeat this process with the rest of your animals, tying them onto the anklet every inch or so. Make 2 anklets—one for each leg!

Animal Cracker Magnets

Decorate these animals in traditional African colors, and put them to work holding up all your Kwanza and holiday greeting cards.

What You'll Need:

animal crackers

permanent markers

clear nail polish

sticky-backed magnetic strip

scissors

Celebrating the traditional African holiday of Kwanza may put you in the mood for an African safari. Create a whole herd of colorful wild animals!

To begin this project, select several animal crackers. Gently color them with markers in the traditional African colors of red, green, and black. Make sure you don't press too hard while you color, unless you want to end up with a headless or tailless beast! Brush a light coat of clear nail polish over the colored crackers; let dry. Turn the crackers over, and coat the backs of the beasts with nail polish, too. Let dry. Cut out a small piece of magnetic strip for each animal, and attach it to the back of the cracker. Again, be careful when you press on the crackers. Stick them on the refrigerator, and admire your beautiful beasts!

DEAR KIDS —
I'LL BE BACK SOON.
DO YOUR HOMEWORK.
LOVE, MOM

Silver Bell Ornaments

Make your own jingle bells to hang from the Christmas tree.

What You'll Need:

cardboard egg carton

scissors

pea-size beads

needle and thread

silver paint and paintbrush

ribbon

Cut out 1 section of an egg carton for each bell. String a bead onto a piece of thread, and secure the bead with a knot. Ask an adult to help you use a needle to poke the free end of the thread through the egg carton section. Knot the end of the thread, making sure the bead swings freely inside the section. When you have made 3 bells, tie them to a longer piece of thread. Paint the bells silver. Tie a ribbon in a bow around the long string. Hang the ornament on your Christmas tree, and gather the family around to sing "Jingle Bells."

Snowy Christmas Cake House

This cake house is as much fun to make as it is to eat!

What You'll Need:

refrigerated pound cake

knife

ruler

plate

white frosting

tiny candy canes, red and green gumdrops, and small thin chocolate squares

toothpicks

Ask an adult to help you cut four 2-inch squares of pound cake. Using a plate as the base, put the squares together in a box shape to make the 4 walls of the house. Use frosting as the mortar that will hold your house together. Cut 2 more squares for the sides of the roof, again using frosting as mortar. Cut another square in half, and use each half to carefully close up the front and back of the roof. Now frost the entire house with white frosting so it looks snowy. You can make a chimney with 3 gumdrops on a toothpick, create doors and windows out of chocolate squares, and then add snow (frosting) all around the house. And don't forget a candy cane fence!

It's never a snowy Christmas in Australia. In fact, it's not unusual for the temperature to reach 100 degrees, so many Australians often have their Christmas dinner at the beach!

Pomander Balls

These traditional spicy-smelling pomanders make great holiday decorations or gifts.

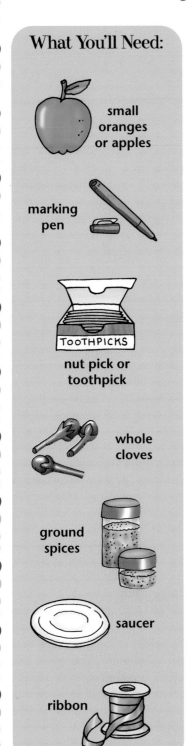

What You'll Need:

small oranges or apples

marking pen

nut pick or toothpick

TOOTHPICKS

whole cloves

ground spices

saucer

ribbon

Select a small, firm apple or orange without bruises. Be sure it is a small one, no more than 3 inches across. (Larger pomanders take a long time to make and may not dry well.) Use a marking pen to divide the surface into about 8 to 10 sections.

Working 1 section at a time, use a nutpick or a toothpick to poke a hole in the fruit's skin. Stick the stem of a whole clove into the hole. Do not poke a lot of holes in the skin and then insert the cloves. Instead, go one at a time so you can see how to fit the cloves together. Be patient. Fill 1 section at a time, allowing gaps between the cloves. The fruit will shrink as it dries, so the gaps will close up.

When the whole fruit is covered, pour ground cinnamon, cloves, nutmeg, or allspice into a saucer, and roll the pomander in it. Allow the pomander to dry in a warm place for 2 weeks. Tie ribbons around it, and hang it up in the kitchen, or give your pomander ball away as a holiday gift.

In some rural parts of the Netherlands, a custom known as Midwinter Horn Blowing is still practiced. Each evening, farmers blow long horns made from elder trees to announce the arrival of Christmas.

Chapter 5

Imagination Station

Invent an Insect

What does a doodlebug look like? It's all in your imagination when you create your own crazy critters!

What You'll Need:

egg carton

scissors

craft glue

decorations
(uncooked pasta,
straws, buttons)

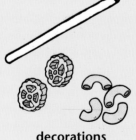

Cut 3 linked sections out of the egg carton to make an insect body. Then glue on the insect's other parts: head, antennae, legs (six, of course), and so on, using uncooked pasta, straws, packing peanuts, buttons—anything you find around the house. What is your bug's name? Does it have a story?

Insects of all shapes and sizes outnumber humans 100 million to one! Did you know that the largest insects that ever lived on Earth were giant dragonflies with wingspans of over 3 feet? Creepy!

Rebus Story

The next time friends come to play, ask them to make their very own rebus story. Then you can exchange stories and read them to each other!

What You'll Need:

black felt-tip pen

drawing paper

markers

stapler

  Create a story with pictures for words. You can make up your own story or use your favorite fairy tale. Write your story on a piece of paper. As you write it down, draw certain words, especially repeated words, as pictures. For example, if you wrote a story about a king, you could draw a picture of a crown as the symbol for the word "king." Write and draw a whole story, and staple the pieces of paper together to make a book.

Once apon a ,

the visited the .

It was the 's birthday.

He ate .

Box Cars

*With a few materials and a little imagination,
you can make a race car, a sports car, or even a minivan.*

What You'll Need:

old, small boxes

scissors

construction paper

craft glue

markers

plastic soda bottle caps

clear plastic cup

aluminum foil

Save some small boxes that are about the size of a butter box, a cocoa mix box, or a necklace box. Cover the boxes with different colors of construction paper. Then decorate the paper-covered boxes with markers. For the wheels, glue on plastic soda bottle caps, or cut out circles from cardboard. To make a windshield, cut a clear plastic cup in half, and glue it to the box. Then use aluminum foil to make headlights and bumpers. If you want, cut holes in the top of the boxes to hold the Clothespin People on page 117. Use them to drive your cars around town.

A lot of race cars, sports cars, and minivans can drive side by side on the Monumental Axis in Brazil. As the world's widest road, it can hold 160 cars driving side by side!

Air Guitar Plus

Playing a rock star has never been easier . . . or more fun!

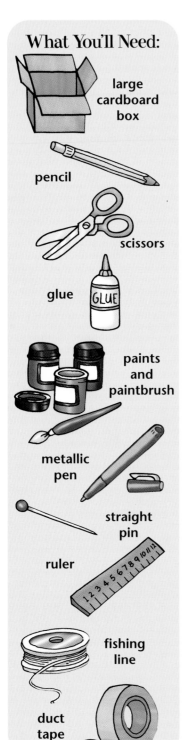

What You'll Need:

large cardboard box

pencil

scissors

glue

paints and paintbrush

metallic pen

straight pin

ruler

fishing line

duct tape

Draw a life-size guitar on one of the long sides of a large cardboard box. Cut out the guitar, then trace around the neck of the guitar on cardboard to make another neck (make this one a bit longer than the original). Cut out the second neck, and glue it to the back of the first neck.

Paint your guitar however you'd like. When the paint is dry, draw frets (the lines along the neck of the guitar) with the metallic pen.

With a straight pin, make 4 small holes along the top of the neck and 4 holes at the bottom third of the guitar's body. Measure from the top holes to the bottom holes, and add 4 inches. Then cut 4 pieces of fishing line that length. Thread a piece of fishing line through the front of a top hole, and tape down the end of the line on the back of the neck with duct tape. Thread the other end through the corresponding hole at the bottom of the guitar. Tape down that end of the line on the back of the body. Repeat these steps for the other holes and other pieces of line.

Magnetic Movie Theater

Invite your friends to a movie—right inside your house!

What You'll Need:

shoe box

construction paper

scissors

glue

markers

old magazines and catalogs

paper clips

magnets

fabric

flashlight

Do you like movies? Why not make up a science-fiction or fantasy movie, such as *The 100-Foot Child Who Saved the World?* To make your movie theater, cover a shoe box (except the lid) with construction paper. You may want to write the name of your theater on the sides of the box.

Next, cut out pictures you want for the background of your movie from old magazines and catalogs. Does your movie take place in a city? Cut out or draw buildings, and glue them to the inside of the box. If you want something to move—people, animals, clouds, or cars—glue a paper clip to the back of the object. When you tell the story of your movie, put your cutout against the background, and press a magnet against the back of the shoe box behind the paper clip. When you let go of the cutout, the magnet will hold it up. You can also cut out fabric curtains and glue the top edge to the top of the box. Turn out the lights before your movie starts, and have a friend shine a flashlight onto the "screen" just as you flip the curtains up. (The illustration above shows the top cut off the box to better show the inside scene.)

Wild & Crazy Monsters

In this project, you begin with a good story and make it even better. It's a test of your imagination.

What You'll Need:

drawing paper

pencil

markers

Read a book about imaginary monsters, such as *Where the Wild Things Are,* and then create your own make-believe creatures. Sketch a fun or scary monster on a piece of paper, and color it in. Or use the drawing technique in The Art of Tracing on page 20 to create an outline of a shape, such as a bear. Turn the shape into a monster by adding horns, sharp teeth, and a tail. Then color it in. Make all kinds of monsters—a giant one, a ghostlike creature, or a dragonlike animal—to create your own picture book.

Moviegoers have always gone crazy for monsters. One of the most famous monsters, Godzilla, was the star of more than 20 movies. That's wild!

Sock Puppets

Make a cast of colorful characters with old socks in bright colors.

What You'll Need:

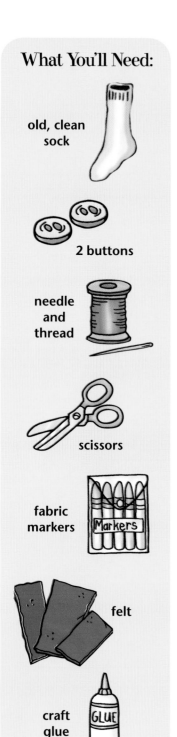

old, clean
sock

2 buttons

needle
and
thread

scissors

fabric
markers

felt

craft
glue

You can make tons of fun puppets out of old socks. Why not try a dragon sock puppet? With an adult's help, sew on button eyes to your sock. Be sure you don't sew through to the other side! Draw 2 eyelash shapes on a piece of felt, and cut them out. Then glue the eyelashes to the sock above the button eyes. Draw a mouth and scales on the dragon with markers. Also draw and cut out the dragon's tongue, wings, and spikes from the felt. Refer to the illustration below, and glue the pieces to the dragon. After you finish your dragon sock puppet, make more puppets with other socks. You could add trims to make a princess and a knight. Use felt pieces for their clothes and features and yarn for their hair. Now you're ready to put on a puppet show!

Picture Perfect

Capture your life and loves in pictures, then share them with the world.

What You'll Need:

camera

poster board

glue

markers

pen

index cards

Work around the house and neighborhood doing chores until you earn enough money to buy a disposable camera and to have the photos developed (or ask a parent if you can borrow his or her camera). Then see if you can tell the story of who you are, using pictures alone.

Are you messy? Take a picture of your room. Do you love animals? Take a photograph of your favorite pet. Take your time, and really make every picture count. Mount your photos on poster board with glue, and write a few words under each picture describing what they say about you. Or write your captions on index cards, and arrange the cards and pictures in a photo album.

Radio Drawing

Turn music into art without opening your mouth!

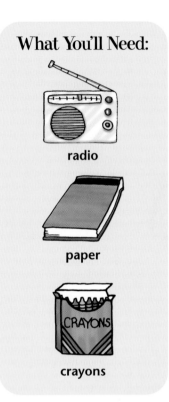

What You'll Need:

radio

paper

crayons

If you listen carefully, music that doesn't have any words can paint a picture in your mind. Turn on the radio, and find a station that is playing music without words. Jazz or classical music works well.

Now close your eyes. How many different instruments can you hear? Do they sound like they're working with each other or against each other? Is one instrument easier to hear than the others? Is the music loud or soft? Does the music sound rushed and crowded, as if everything is hurrying to get to the next note? Or is it slow and lazy, as if the notes were taking a walk along the beach at sunset? What about the mood of the music? Does it sound happy? Sad? Sleepy? Excited?

Now think about what colors match the music that you're hearing. If the sounds were shapes on a page, what would they look like? Draw what you think the music would look like.

Clothespin People

Create your own action figures—family members, superheroes, or even an Olympic ski team!

What You'll Need:

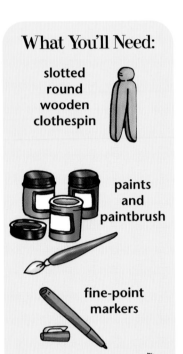

slotted round wooden clothespin

paints and paintbrush

fine-point markers

chenille stem

craft glue

felt

scissors

construction paper

Before you begin this project, cover your work surface. Paint on clothes for your clothespin person, letting the paint dry between each section. First paint the bottom ½ inch of the clothespin for the shoes. Then paint the slotted "legs" for the pants. To make a shirt, paint the top part of the clothespin body. (Leave the knob unpainted.) Draw a face on the knob of the clothespin using fine-point markers. To make the arms, wrap a chenille stem around the middle of the shirt, and glue it in place. Cut out a hat from felt, and glue it on top of the head. You could also cut small paper skis out of construction paper, and glue them to the bottom of the clothespin legs. You'll have so much fun making 1 clothespin person that you'll want to make a whole bunch!

You already know that clothespins can be used for much more than hanging wet laundry. But did you know that the famous inventor Stanley Mason, the inventor of the first disposable diaper and the squeezable ketchup bottle, also invented a clothespin fishing lure?

Flying Machines

People have dreamed of flying ever since... well, ever since there have been people. Now it's your turn to make a flying machine!

What You'll Need:

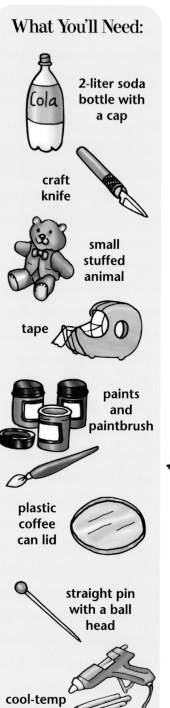

2-liter soda bottle with a cap

craft knife

small stuffed animal

tape

paints and paintbrush

plastic coffee can lid

straight pin with a ball head

cool-temp glue gun

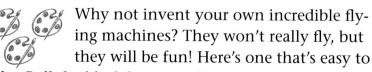

Why not invent your own incredible flying machines? They won't really fly, but they will be fun! Here's one that's easy to make: Pull the black bottom off of a 2-liter soda bottle. Have an adult cut the bottle in half with a craft knife. Set a stuffed animal "pilot" in the top of the bottle. Push the top of the soda bottle into the base to make the body of your flying machine (with the pilot inside). Wrap tape around the seam between the top and the base. Paint the machine, leaving the top front half clear for the windshield. Have an adult help you cut 4 sections out of a coffee can lid—don't cut the rim! Push the pin through the center of the coffee can lid and into the center of the soda pop lid. With an adult's help, paint and then glue the plastic lid cutouts on as wings for your airplane. Happy flying!

Mighty Masks

These easy-to-make masks look hilarious!

What You'll Need:

old magazines

scissors

thin
paper plates

glue

pencil

yarn

Leaf through old magazines, and cut out individual features from pictures of faces. Don't forget animal faces! Divide the features into piles of ears, noses, eyebrows, chins, hair, etc.

Now cut eye and mouth holes out of a paper plate. Pick out a goofy arrangement of facial features, and glue them onto the plate to make a mask. Let the glue dry. Next, punch holes in the sides of the mask with a pencil. Tie a piece of yarn through the hole on each side to hold the mask on your head. You'll roar at the crazy results!

African masks have been very important throughout history. Many African masks are created to show different animals, such as lions or elephants. Dancers wear the masks for special celebrations, and sometimes the masks are even worn to help plants grow!

A Grandparent's Story

When you combine your drawing with a grandparent's story, you create a generational piece of artwork.

What You'll Need:

3×5-inch index cards

pencil

construction paper

glue

markers

hole punch

yarn

 Make a book about your grandparents. Think of a question, and write it on an index card. Try to come up with 8 to 10 questions. You can ask questions such as "What was your favorite toy?" or "Where did you live when you were 10?" Have them write the answer on the card. If your grandparents live far away, mail the cards back and forth.

Once you have all the cards, glue each one to the bottom half of a sheet of construction paper. Draw a picture above the card to illustrate your grandparent's answer. Then decorate a separate sheet of construction paper for the front cover. To bind your book, set all the pages together, and punch 4 holes along the left edge. Cut a piece of yarn, thread it through the holes, and tie it in a bow.

What was your favorite toy?

A train

Brainteaser Art

Make a brainteaser for your friends to figure out, while creating wonderful art!

What You'll Need:

paper

stencil shapes (available at office supply, craft, or art stores)

pencil

markers

Use a stencil to create pictures out of geometric designs. Try a butterfly with lots of circles within circles or a house with squares for windows, shutters, chimneys, and even bricks. Keep track of the number of shapes you have drawn. If you want, use markers to make your brainteaser a kaleidoscope of color. Be sure to count the shapes as you draw your picture, or you could end up teasing yourself! When you're finished with your drawing, challenge a friend or family member to count the shapes.

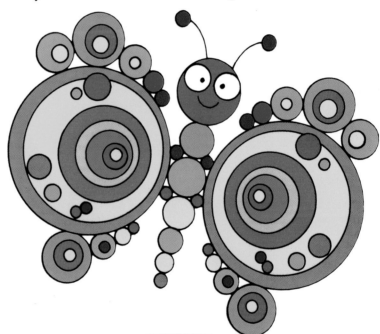

Your brain is the control center for millions of signals from the nerves in your body. In fact, 1 human brain generates more electric impulses in a single day than all of the world's telephones put together!

Gourd Puppets

Pick out some funny-shape gourds, make puppets, and put on a show!

What You'll Need:

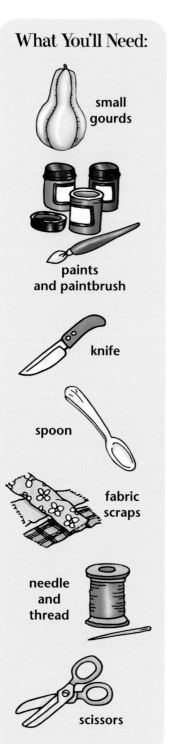

small gourds

paints and paintbrush

knife

spoon

fabric scraps

needle and thread

scissors

 You can pick gourds fresh from a garden or find them in markets during the fall or winter.

To make a gourd finger puppet: Using the long, curved top of the gourd as the nose, paint on features for a face. Have an adult help you cut a hole in the bottom of the puppet's "head" and scoop out the contents with a spoon. Allow the gourd to dry, then use your finger as the puppet's neck.

To make a gourd hand puppet: Turn the gourd upside-down, and use the long, curved part as the neck. Then paint a funny face on the "head." You could also sew clothes for your puppet from fabric scraps.

Now it's time for the show!

Cartoon Evolution

What happens when you mix Superman and Bugs Bunny?

What You'll Need:

newspapers, comic books, magazines, and old picture books

scissors

glue

white paper

pencil

Everyone loves cartoon characters. There's just something about them that makes us laugh out loud. But what happens when you mix an old favorite with a new friend? Fun, that's what! And this craft adventure will show you how.

Go through newspapers, comic books, magazines, and picture books, and cut out a bunch of different pictures of cartoon characters. Set all the pictures out on a table, just to see exactly what you've found. Glue your favorite character to a sheet of paper. Then see what kinds of updates you can make. Is Mickey Mouse on the page? Why not give him Spider-Man's pants? Or add a little feline fluff by tacking on Garfield's tail. Is Mickey hungry? Maybe he'd like a taste of Popeye's spinach. Get creative. Then write a story about your new friend.

Hawaiian Hula Skirt

You can learn to dance the hula, but it just doesn't look right unless you have a "grass" skirt. Make this simple skirt, and start dancing!

What You'll Need:

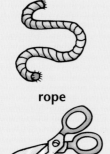

rope

scissors

green raffia

Measure the rope around your waist, and add a few extra inches before cutting. Then take a piece of green raffia, and hang it from the rope so the ends are even. Tie a knot to hold the raffia in place. Keep adding and tying pieces of raffia onto the rope until it looks like a grass skirt. When the rope is covered (except for the extra inches), tie it around your waist.

Now it's time for hula dancing! The hula is a dance with hand movements that tell a story. You may not have classes in your area to learn how to hula dance, but you can make up your own stories. Act them out with your hands, and move your body in a rhythmic pattern.

Teach a few of your friends your new-style hula, then put on a show for the neighborhood or your families!

Hawaiian hula dancers often wear leis, which are braided or woven necklaces made of natural material like flowers or shells. That's because the lei is the traditional offering to Laka, goddess of the dance. Leis are also given to people when they visit Hawaii to symbolize friendship.

Felt Storyboards

*Turn a pizza box into a storyboard,
and bring the story to life with felt pictures.*

What You'll Need:

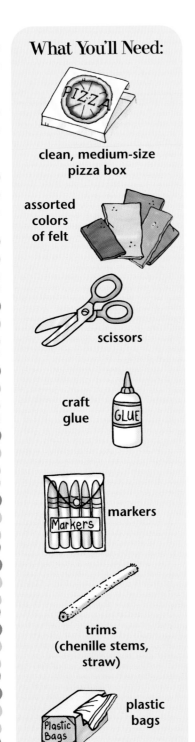

clean, medium-size
pizza box

assorted
colors
of felt

scissors

craft
glue

markers

trims
(chenille stems,
straw)

plastic
bags

To make the storyboard background, cut 2 pieces of felt to fit the insides of the top and bottom of the pizza box. Apply a layer of glue to the inside of the box at the top and bottom. Place both felt background pieces down in the box over the glue. Let the glue set.

Using assorted colors of felt, cut out different objects to make a picture. For example, if you were telling the story "The Three Little Pigs," you would need 3 pig cutouts, 1 wolf cutout, and 3 house cutouts. Use markers to draw the features on your cutouts, such as the eyes, noses, and mouths on the little pigs. Then glue on cutout felt overalls, and use small pieces of curled chenille stem for the tails. Decorate each house with markers, felt, and other trims. Glue a bit of straw or some twigs on 1 house and red felt bricks to another house.

Place your pieces on the felt background to tell your story. When you're done playing with the story board, store each set of pieces in a plastic bag, and place the bags in your pizza box.

Stretch and Wreck Cars

Invent a car with a pool in the backseat, or design a futuristic car. Let your imagination go full speed!

What You'll Need:

old magazines

scissors

craft glue

drawing or construction paper

markers

Cut out cars and other vehicles from magazine ads. Cut the cars into separate pieces (doors, tires, windshields, etc.). Then mix and match the pieces to make your own creative vehicle. Glue the different parts together to create crazy combinations. For example, you could add more door parts between the front and back of a car to make a limo. Or glue extra-big tires on a small car. Another idea is to add a bus front to a luxury car back. Once you've created your crazy combination, glue it on a piece of drawing or construction paper. Then draw a scene around your vehicle.

There are almost 500 million cars around the world. The United States, with less than 10 percent of the world's population, owns 30 percent of the world's cars! That's because the typical American family has 2 to 3 cars that each log in about 5,000 miles per year.

Kool Kazoo

You don't need years of practice to make beautiful music.
All you need is this kazoo and a good song to hum!

What You'll Need:

paper towel tube

markers

waxed paper

rubber band

scissors

Decorate a paper towel tube with markers. Then wrap a piece of waxed paper over 1 end of the tube. Secure the waxed paper with a rubber band. Carefully cut 2 holes in the top of the tube. Space the holes out a bit so they're not right on top of each other.

To play your kazoo, hum your favorite song into the open end of the tube. Cover and uncover the 2 holes with your fingers to make different sounds. To make other interesting sounds, make more kazoos with tubes that have different diameters, thicknesses, and lengths, such as a short toilet paper tube or a long wrapping paper tube.

Did you know that January 28 is National Kazoo Day? That would be a great day to hear Rick Hubbard, known as the King of Kazoo, perform in concert. When Rick performs, he gives free kazoos to everyone in the audience!

Magic Wand

*With a wave of the magic wand,
you can become a magician or even a fairy godmother!*

What You'll Need:

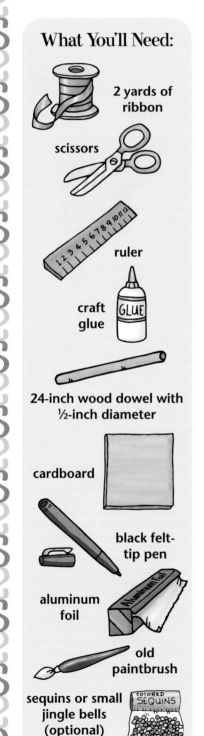

2 yards of ribbon

scissors

ruler

craft glue

24-inch wood dowel with ½-inch diameter

cardboard

black felt-tip pen

aluminum foil

old paintbrush

sequins or small jingle bells (optional)

Cut a 24-inch piece of ribbon. Glue 1 end of the ribbon to 1 end of the wood dowel. Wrap it around the dowel. Once you reach the bottom, trim off the excess ribbon, and glue the end in place. To make the wand streamers, cut a few strips of ribbon with varying lengths. Glue 1 end of each strip to the top end of the dowel. If you want, add some sequins or small jingle bells to each streamer end.

Next, cut a small strip of cardboard about 1 inch long. Wrap and glue the strip of cardboard around the dowel ½ inch from the top end. The strip will extend beyond the dowel but should cover the ends of the ribbons. Cut 2 small slits in the cardboard across from each other. Draw and cut out a moon, a star, or another magical symbol from the aluminum foil. To stiffen the foil shape, use an old paintbrush to coat 1 side with glue, and let it dry. Insert the foil shape in the slits. Add a dab of glue to hold it in place.

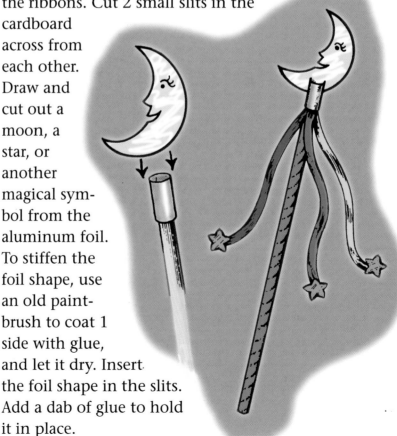

Pretend Store

Invite your friends over, and have each of them design their own store.
Together you can make a mini-mall.

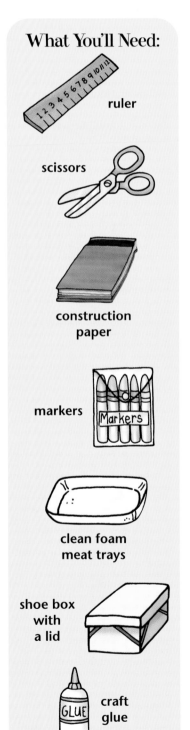

What You'll Need:

ruler

scissors

construction paper

markers

clean foam meat trays

shoe box with a lid

craft glue

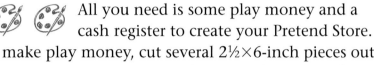 All you need is some play money and a cash register to create your Pretend Store. To make play money, cut several 2½×6-inch pieces out of green construction paper. Decorate them to make your own paper money. Add the amounts—$1, $5, $10, and even $100. Then cut several circles from foam meat trays to make coins. Decorate them with markers.

Make a cash register from a shoe box by first cutting the lid in half. Use one half as the cash drawer. Place the lid half back on the box, and turn the box upside down. Pull out the lid, and place your play money inside. To make the cash register buttons, cut out small circles from different colors of construction paper, and glue them to the box.

Now you're ready to play store. For a grocery store, gather food cartons and boxes. Use stuffed animals for a pet store. Draw your store's sign on a piece of construction paper, and display it to tell everyone you're open for business!

Design a Menu

Imagine a restaurant that serves silly food.
Then invent a fun menu for your new restaurant.

What You'll Need:

construction paper

black felt-tip pen

markers

magazines

scissors

glue

To design a menu for your new restaurant, fold a large piece of construction paper in half lengthwise. Write your items on the menu, and decorate it to match your restaurant theme. You could make the menu silly with chicken everything—chicken soup, chicken desserts, and even chicken drinks. You can even add outrageous prices for your silly dishes.

If you don't want a silly menu, make a real one with your favorite dishes. Use magazines or a grocery store circular to cut and paste food pictures on the menu. Then play a game of restaurant with your friends. Gather some play dishes, a tray, and an apron. Draw order forms on a piece of paper. Give your friends a menu, and take their orders.

Fancy Boa

A boa is a glamorous accessory.
Here's one you can make the next time you play dress up.

What You'll Need:

plastic needlepoint
needle

yarn

scissors

2 yards of
tulle netting

glitter or sequins
(optional)

craft glue
(optional)

Thread a needle with about 4 feet of yarn, and tie a knot at 1 end. Cut all the tulle netting into 4-inch-wide strips. Then use the needle and yarn to sew a gathering stitch through 1 strip of the netting. Thread the yarn in and out in even stitches about 1 inch apart down the center of the netting. Every yard or so, pull the yarn rather tightly to bunch up the netting. Continue stitching onto more strips until you have used all the netting strips. Trim off the excess yarn, and tie it in a knot. Spread the netting out evenly. If you want to add sparkle to your boa, glue on glitter or sequins.

Chapter 6

Nature in the Neighborhood

Pebble Sculptures

All it takes is a little imagination to turn ordinary pebbles into extraordinary art!

What You'll Need:

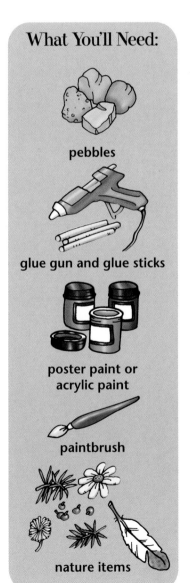

pebbles

glue gun and glue sticks

poster paint or acrylic paint

paintbrush

nature items

If you have a collection of ordinary rocks that you don't know what to do with, try making sculptures out of them. Lay out your rocks, and look for interesting features that might suggest human or animal faces, heads, arms, legs, or bodies. A large, smooth rock might make you think of a beetle. A heart-shape rock could be part of a pebble valentine. Glue the rocks together with thick, sticky glue. (Hot glue works best, but be sure to have an adult help you with the glue gun.) Once the glue has dried, use acrylic paints or poster paints to add color to your figures. Be original!

Decorate your rock sculptures with other natural things you find. An acorn cap makes a good hat. Feathers that you find in the grass can become tails for your pebble birds. White thistledown or cotton from cotton- woods can make white Santa Claus beards and hair.

A Visual "Diary"

You'll remember your next nature trip long after it's over when you create this "natural wonders" wall hanging.

What You'll Need:

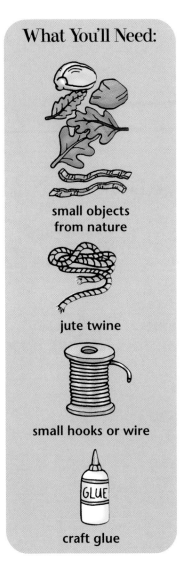

small objects from nature

jute twine

small hooks or wire

GLUE

craft glue

When you go on a nature hike, collect small objects such as twigs, grasses, flowers, nuts, bark, and shells. (Be sure to collect at least 4 twigs or sticks; you'll need these to complete your Visual Diary.) When you get home, you can weave all the objects together to make an artistic record of your trip.

First, make a frame for your artwork. Tie together 4 twigs or sticks to make a square or rectangle. Next, wrap natural jute twine around the frame. Use the twine as a base on which to mount all the other objects. You can weave them through the twine, use small hooks or pieces of wire to hook them on, or glue them on. You could attach the objects to the frame in the order you found them or in an artistic design. Either way, you'll have a unique "diary" of your trip.

Leafy Bleach Prints

Use "reverse" bleach prints to make beautiful greeting cards.

What You'll Need:

rubber gloves

smock or apron

colored paper

bleach

small glass dish

paintbrush or cotton swab

assortment of leaves

markers

Caution: Bleach can irritate skin and eyes. Wear rubber gloves when doing this project, and have an adult help you.

Before you begin this project, cover your work surface. Also put on a smock or an apron to protect your clothes from the bleach. Lay out a sheet of colored paper on your work surface. Have an adult help you pour a little bleach into a small glass dish. Use an old paintbrush or a cotton swab to paint the back of a leaf with bleach, then press the leaf bleach side down on the paper. Lift off the leaf. In a moment or two you will see a bleached-out print of the leaf.

After you have made a nice arrangement of prints on the paper, you can hang it up as a picture. Or fold the paper in half, and decorate it with markers to make a greeting card.

Rainy-Day Pictures

Create your own masterpiece—with a little help from the rain!

What You'll Need:

paper

water-soluble paint
and paintbrush
or markers

You've probably used lots of things to create works of art, like paint, markers, tissue paper, string, and even rocks. But have you ever used the rain to create artwork? This idea may sound all wet, but give it a try!

Use your paint or markers to draw a picture on a piece of paper. Then bring on the rain! Place your piece of paper in the rain for about 20 seconds. When you take your "canvas" out of the rain, let it dry, and then look at your creation. Thanks to the rain, your picture will have turned into something else entirely!

Does it seem like it always rains on Saturdays but seldom on Mondays? Some scientists think that air pollution, caused by factories and the cars of people going to work, builds toward the weekend, increasing the chances for rain.

Natural Bookmarks

Create truly individual bookmarks using the beauty of plants.
They make great gifts for your favorite bookworms.

What You'll Need:

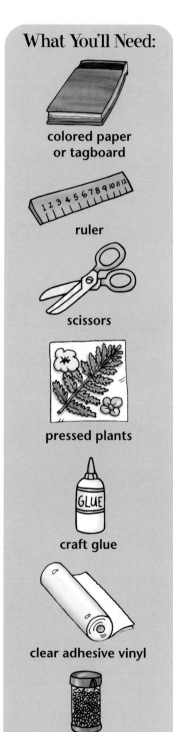

colored paper
or tagboard

ruler

scissors

pressed plants

craft glue

clear adhesive vinyl

glitter (optional)

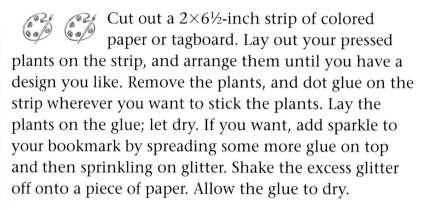 Cut out a 2×6½-inch strip of colored paper or tagboard. Lay out your pressed plants on the strip, and arrange them until you have a design you like. Remove the plants, and dot glue on the strip wherever you want to stick the plants. Lay the plants on the glue; let dry. If you want, add sparkle to your bookmark by spreading some more glue on top and then sprinkling on glitter. Shake the excess glitter off onto a piece of paper. Allow the glue to dry.

Next, cut out a piece of clear adhesive vinyl about 4×6½ inches. Carefully peel off the backing, and lay it flat, sticky-side up, on a table. (You may need an adult to help you with this.) Turn your bookmark over so that the decorated side is down, and lay it in the middle of the clear adhesive vinyl. Then fold the rest of the vinyl over to cover the back. Trim the ends, leaving a small margin of clear adhesive vinyl.

Critters-in-Holes

Critters you can eat: Yummy!
You'll love making—and eating—these sweet, gooey treats!

What You'll Need:

shortening

muffin tins

48 chewy caramel candies
coated in chocolate

knife

48 pieces of
candy corn

vanilla icing

1 package (20 ounces)
of refrigerated peanut
butter cookie dough

Before you begin making your critters, pre-heat the oven to 350°F, and grease twelve 1¾-inch muffin cups with shortening.

Have an adult help you cut a slit into the side of 1 caramel candy. Then carefully insert a piece of candy corn into the slit. Repeat with the remaining caramel candies and candy corn. To create eyes for your critter, dot icing on top of each piece of candy.

Next, remove the cookie dough from its wrapper, and have an adult help you cut the dough into 12 equal slices. Then cut each slice into 4 equal sections. Place 1 section of dough into each muffin cup.

Bake the cookie dough for 9 minutes. Remove the cookies from the oven, and immediately press 1 decorated caramel candy into the center of each cookie. Take the cookies out of the muffin tin, and let them cool completely. Repeat until you've baked and decorated all the cookies. Makes 4 dozen "critters."

Rose Beads

These lovely beads, which were popular in Victorian times for making necklaces and rosaries, will keep their scent for decades.

What You'll Need:

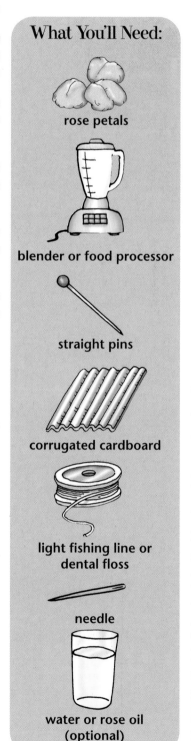

rose petals

blender or food processor

straight pins

corrugated cardboard

light fishing line or dental floss

needle

water or rose oil (optional)

 If someone in your family has some old rose beads, you know how long they stay sweet-smelling! Now, these beads are easier than ever to make, thanks to today's kitchen appliances.

Pick roses early in the morning before the sun drives off some of the scent. Choose roses with similar scents, or blend scents that go well together. Most colors will blend well, as the beads will all darken to a mahogany color.

Ask an adult to put 1 handful of petals at a time in a blender or food processor; blend them until you have a thick paste. You may add a few drops of water, if needed, or even a bit of rose oil. If necessary, you can spoon the paste into a jar and keep it refrigerated while you wait for more roses to bloom.

When you have enough paste, roll it into pea-size beads. Run a pin through each bead, and stick the pin into a piece of corrugated cardboard. Let the beads dry thoroughly. Then use a needle to string the beads on light fishing line or dental floss. Tie the ends of the fishing line together to make a necklace, bracelet, or other beaded beauty!

Down-to-Earth Stars

Twig stars make terrific natural holiday tree ornaments. Here are 2 different kinds of stars you can make to decorate your tree, a window, or any place!

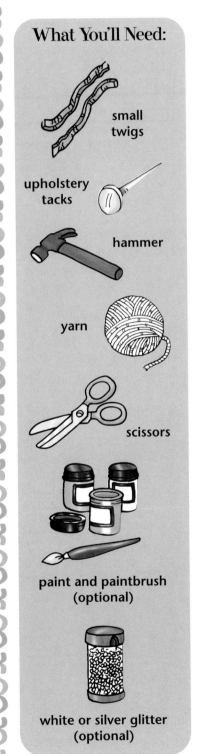

What You'll Need:

small twigs

upholstery tacks

hammer

yarn

scissors

paint and paintbrush (optional)

white or silver glitter (optional)

To make a 5-pointed twig star: You'll need 5 twigs, several inches long, all the same length. Lay them in the shape of a 5-pointed star. Use gold or silver upholstery tacks to attach the twigs at each point. The tacks not only hold the star together but also add a pretty, shining touch. For a really shiny star, paint the twigs with metallic gold or silver paint before you tack them together.

To make a 6-pointed twig star: You'll need 3 twigs, several inches long, all the same length. Cross the 3 twigs in the middle so they make a shape like a 6-pointed star. Wrap the twigs with yarn to hold them together, beginning at the center where all 3 twigs meet. Wrap the yarn around 1 stick, then the next, and then the next. Keep wrapping the yarn (it will make a sort of bull's-eye pattern) until it is close to the ends of the sticks. When you're finished, tie the yarn in the back.

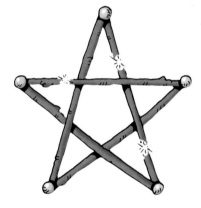

You can use different colors of yarn on the same star to make a colorful design. Or turn your star into a snowflake by painting the twigs white, wrapping them with white yarn, and adding white or silver glitter.

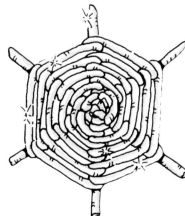

Clamshell Garden

Collect clams on a beach—or visit your local fish market—
to create your own miniature garden.

What You'll Need:

clam half-shell

small cactus

GLUE — craft glue

sand — Colored Sand

small pebbles (no larger than ⅛-inch in diameter)

moss

potting soil

GRASS SEED — seeds

To make a cactus garden: Place a tiny variety of cactus inside the clamshell, using a small amount of glue to hold it in place. Fill the shell with a mixture of half sand and half tiny pebbles and moss. Dampen the mixture, and place the shell in a sunny spot. Your garden should be watered once a week. Be careful not to overwater it!

To make a seed garden: Sprinkle tiny pebbles along the bottom of the clamshell, followed by ½ inch of potting soil. Spread moss on top. Dampen and sprinkle some seeds (grass seeds work well, or you can try alfalfa, clover, mustard seed, radish, or rye) on top of the moss. Layer more soil over the seeds and moss. Water your garden lightly, and keep it in a dark place until the seeds sprout. Then move it to a sunny spot.

Butterfly Net

*Examine beautiful butterflies and other small creatures
with help from this easy-to-make net.*

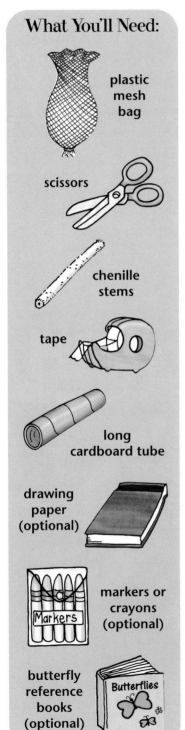

What You'll Need:

plastic mesh bag

scissors

chenille stems

tape

long cardboard tube

drawing paper (optional)

markers or crayons (optional)

Markers

butterfly reference books (optional)

Butterflies

Cut the clamp off the end of a mesh onion bag (leave 1 end clamped). Next, make a rim for the net by twisting together the ends of 2 chenille stems. Thread the stems in and out along the top edge of the mesh bag. When you're finished, secure the ends of the rim with a piece of tape.

For a handle, use a very stiff cardboard tube (like the kind found in a roll of wrapping paper). On 1 end of the tube, cut a slit on each side. Then insert the rim of the net into the slits, and tape it in place.

Now it's time to go out and explore the natural world. When you find and capture a butterfly, examine it quickly, and then draw it. After you let the butterfly go, you can look up the butterfly in a book to determine what type it is and to learn more about it. Collect several pages of drawings, and make your own butterfly book.

You'll be a butterfly expert in no time!

Ice Hangings

When the weather turns cold, you can make these temporary but beautiful natural decorations.

What You'll Need:

pie pan

water

yarn

scissors

nature objects
(flowers, berries,
evergreen sprigs)

Fill a pie pan with water, and line the edge with yarn, making sure the yarn is submerged in the water. Leave the ends of the yarn loose, so you can hang up your project when it's finished.

Next, arrange some nature objects in the center of the pan. You can use fresh or dried flowers, greenery, berries, or anything you like. If the temperature outside is below freezing, set your pie pan outdoors. Or you can place it in the freezer. Wait until the yarn and flowers are frozen completely into the ice before bringing the pie pan indoors or removing it from the freezer.

Once it is frozen, you can remove the ice circle from the pan. (Dip the bottom of the pan in warm water if you're having trouble removing it.) Now hang it up outdoors on a tree, post, or anywhere its beauty can be seen. Watch your creation sparkle in the sun. As long as the temperatures stay below freezing, your ice hanging won't melt away.

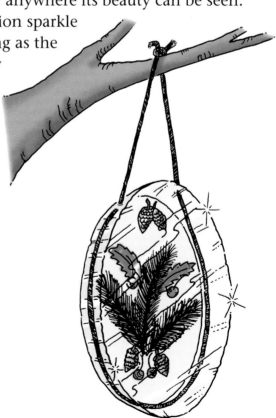

What a Doll!

Corn husk dolls were made by Native Americans in what is now the northeastern United States. Here's how you can make one.

What You'll Need:

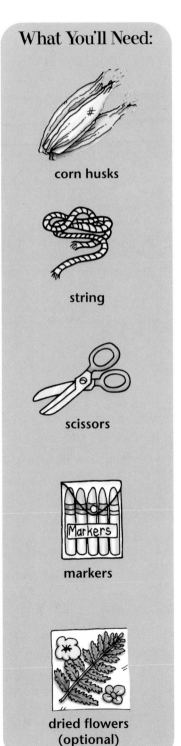

corn husks

string

scissors

markers

dried flowers
(optional)

 Strip the husks from several ears of corn. Let them dry out for a few days. Keep some of the corn silk to use for hair.

First, roll up 1 husk, and put some corn silk on top of the roll. Then wrap another corn husk over the silk and the rolled-up husk. Use string to tie this piece tightly under the rolled-up husk. This will be the head and neck.

Roll a husk lengthwise to make the arms. Tie the long roll at each end. Put this roll under the neck, and tie it in place.

Use several husks to make a skirt. Lay these husks in the front and back of the arms, and tie them in place. Trim the bottom of the skirt so it is even.

To make a blouse, cut a rectangle out of a husk. Then make a cut in 1 end of the rectangle (the cut should go about halfway through the rectangle). Put the rectangle behind the doll, with the cut end up. The end of the rectangle that is not cut will be the back of the blouse.

Fold the cut end of the rectangle over to the front of the doll. This will be the front of the blouse. Cross the 2 flaps over each other, and use string to tie the blouse in place.

Finally, draw a face on your corn husk doll. You can put dried flowers in its hand or make a bonnet for its head out of corn husks, too!

Pebble Mosaic

You've probably seen magnificent mosaics made from glass and stone in a church or museum. Now you can make your own version from pebbles!

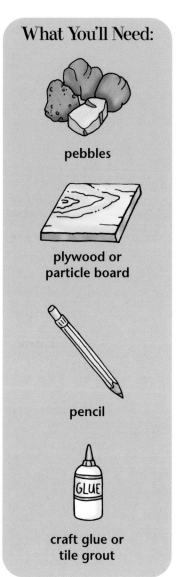

What You'll Need:

pebbles

plywood or particle board

pencil

craft glue or tile grout

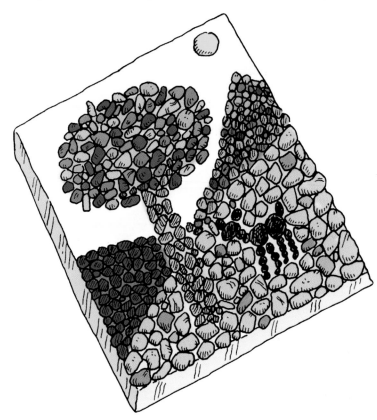

Before you can begin working on your mosaic, you'll need to collect lots of pretty pebbles in different colors and shapes.

If you like, first use a pencil to draw a design on a piece of plywood. Then glue the pebbles on the design. Or spread grout on the plywood, and push the pebbles into the grout.

A pebble mosaic makes a good trivet (used to hold hot pots). You can also make pebble mosaics to decorate flowerpots, vases, or lamps. What else could you decorate with pebbles?

Robin's Egg Treats

Robin Redbreast's eggs don't taste like jellybeans, but these "eggs" do!

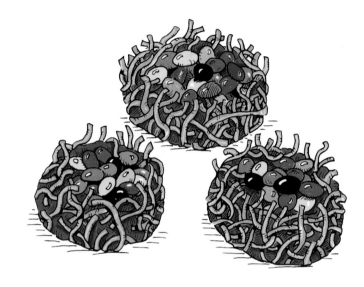

What You'll Need:

- 1⅓ cups of shredded coconut
- cookie sheets
- 3 bowls
- 1 cup of butter, softened
- ½ cup of sugar
- 1 egg
- ½ teaspoon of lemon extract
- 2 cups of all-purpose flour
- ½ teaspoon of salt
- ½ teaspoon of orange peel
- shortening
- 1 cup of small jellybeans

Be sure to ask an adult to help you with this project. First, preheat the oven to 300°F. Spread the coconut on an ungreased cookie sheet, and bake for about 25 minutes or until the coconut begins to brown, stirring occasionally. Put the toasted coconut in a bowl.

Next, increase the oven temperature to 350°F. Beat the butter and sugar in a large bowl until it becomes fluffy. Add the egg and lemon extract; beat until smooth. Combine the flour, salt, and orange peel in a medium bowl. Then add the flour mixture to the butter mixture, and blend well.

Separate the dough into 36 small balls, then roll each ball in toasted coconut until it's completely covered. Place each dough ball 2 inches apart on greased cookie sheets. Using your thumb, make a dent in the center of each ball.

Bake 12 to 14 minutes or until coconut is golden brown. Remove the "nests" to wire racks, and cool completely. Put jellybean "eggs" in the indentations of the cooled cookies. Makes 3 dozen treats.

Snow Painting

Art on a snowy canvas—how cool!

What You'll Need:

food coloring

water

old bowls

paintbrushes

The next time your world turns into a winter wonderland of white, add a little color of your own. Find an old bowl that can get dirty, and combine about 10 drops of food coloring in any shade with about 3 teaspoons of water. (Use 1 bowl for each color you want to make.) Carry your colorful "paint" outside.

Firmly pack a 4×4-foot section of snow to make your "canvas." Now, use your paintbrushes to splash bright colors onto the snow to create an abstract splash. Or paint your favorite characters right on the snow. Be sure to wear old clothes that you can get dirty, because food coloring doesn't wash out of most fabrics.

While it's true that no two are exactly alike, snowflakes can be broken down into 6 different 6-sided crystal categories: needles, columns, plates, columns capped with plates, dendrites, and stars.

Harvest Place Mats

Create decorative place mats that symbolize harvest time.

What You'll Need:

fruits and vegetables
(onion, apple, mushroom)

knife

clean foam
meat trays

paint

construction paper

clear adhesive vinyl

scissors

  Make these festive mealtime decorations by printing with fruits and vegetables.

Start by selecting several fruits and vegetables and cutting each in half. (Have an adult help you with the cutting.) Next, cover your work surface, and pour several colors of paint into clean foam meat trays. Choose fall colors, or create your own personal color scheme.

Dip the cut side of a fruit or vegetable into the paint, and make a print on a sheet of construction paper. Make several prints on the paper. You can cover each sheet of paper with a combination of fruit and vegetable prints or a single fruit printed with different colors. Let the paint dry, then seal the place mats in clear adhesive vinyl.

To seal, cut 2 pieces of clear adhesive vinyl slightly larger than the construction paper place mat. Peel the backing off of 1 sheet of adhesive vinyl, and place it on a table, sticky side up. Carefully lay the place mat on top of the adhesive vinyl, and rub gently so it sticks. Then peel the backing off of the second sheet of adhesive vinyl, and carefully place it, sticky side down, on top of the unsealed side of the place mat. Gently rub to seal, and trim the edges if necessary. Now the easy-to-clean place mats are ready for a holiday meal!

Lunch Bag Kite

Make your own paper bag kite as a way to join in the sky festivities that take place all around the globe!

What You'll Need:

- yarn or string
- yardstick
- scissors
- masking tape or stapler
- lunch-size paper bag
- crayons or markers
- ribbon, wrapping paper, or tissue paper
- glue
- crepe paper streamer

Kites were invented 3,000 years ago in China, and they spread around the world from there. Today, kites and kite festivals are a part of the traditions of many countries, including Guatemala, Japan, India, and Malaysia.

To make a lunch bag kite, cut five 1-yard-long pieces of yarn or string. Take 4 of the pieces of yarn, and tape or staple each one to a corner of the open side of the bag. Tie the loose ends of the 4 pieces together. Tie the fifth piece (for holding the kite) to the end of the 4 knotted strings. Decorate the bag with crayons or markers and by gluing on ribbon, wrapping paper, or tissue paper. Attach a streamer to the bag's bottom, and run with it!

Pinecone Flowers

With a little creativity, you can turn ordinary pinecones into pretty flower decorations.

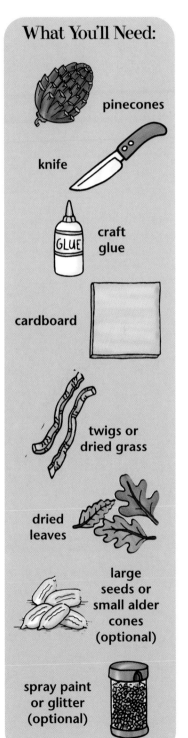

What You'll Need:

pinecones

knife

craft glue

cardboard

twigs or dried grass

dried leaves

large seeds or small alder cones (optional)

spray paint or glitter (optional)

Collect several small pinecones, and brush off any dirt or leaves. If the cones are closed, dry them in a warm oven for several hours until they open.

Ask an adult to cut the pinecones in half. Use a large blob of strong glue to attach the cut halves of the pinecones to a piece of cardboard. Glue on twigs or dried grass to represent flower stems, then glue dried leaves on the twigs. Let the glue dry completely.

You can make smaller flowers by pulling the bracts from the cones and gluing them individually to the board in a flower shape. Use a large seed or a tiny alder cone for a center.

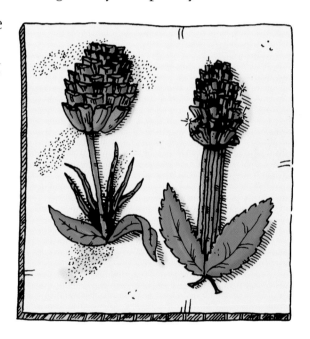

Pinecone flowers look nice plain, but they can be dressed up with silver or gold paint for holiday decorations. (Have an adult help you with the spray paint, and work in a well-ventilated area.) You could also dip the cones in glue, then roll them in glitter before gluing to the board.

Mini Terrarium

Make a little terrarium in a plastic cup, and watch tiny greenery grow!

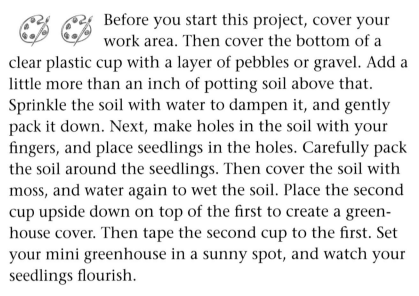 Before you start this project, cover your work area. Then cover the bottom of a clear plastic cup with a layer of pebbles or gravel. Add a little more than an inch of potting soil above that. Sprinkle the soil with water to dampen it, and gently pack it down. Next, make holes in the soil with your fingers, and place seedlings in the holes. Carefully pack the soil around the seedlings. Then cover the soil with moss, and water again to wet the soil. Place the second cup upside down on top of the first to create a greenhouse cover. Then tape the second cup to the first. Set your mini greenhouse in a sunny spot, and watch your seedlings flourish.

clear tape

seedling

moss

soil

gravel

Sun Portraits

*Calling all Picassos! See what happens
when you use the sun to draw a self-portrait.*

What You'll Need:

large piece
of paper

rocks

markers or paints

nature items
(leaves, sticks, seeds)

glue

On a sunny morning, place a large piece of paper on the ground (you may need to tape several pieces of paper together to make 1 big piece). Put some rocks on the corners of the paper to keep it from blowing away. Stand next to the paper so your shadow falls on it. Then have a friend trace the outline of your shadow onto the page. You can do the same for your friend.

Now you're ready to get a little creative with your shadowy self. Using markers or paints, color in your shadow outline, or make crazy designs inside of it. You could also make a collage inside your shadow outline using nature items such as leaves, seeds, sticks, or whatever else you find around the yard. Come back to your creation later in the day, and have a friend trace another shadow next to the one traced earlier. Since the sun is in a different place in the sky, your shadow will have a whole new look!

Precious Belongings Pouch

Make this pouch to carry all the precious belongings you'll collect as you go exploring on field trips or nature walks.

What You'll Need:

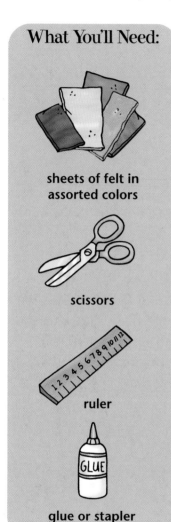

sheets of felt in assorted colors

scissors

ruler

glue or stapler

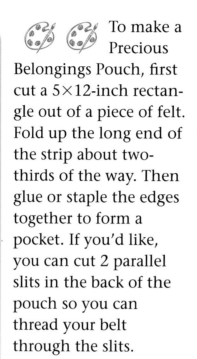

To make a Precious Belongings Pouch, first cut a 5×12-inch rectangle out of a piece of felt. Fold up the long end of the strip about two-thirds of the way. Then glue or staple the edges together to form a pocket. If you'd like, you can cut 2 parallel slits in the back of the pouch so you can thread your belt through the slits.

Next, decorate the pocket by cutting out shapes from the felt and gluing them to the pocket. You could use nature shapes, such as leaves, animals, and flowers, or create an abstract design with a variety of geometric shapes. Now it's time for that nature walk!

Next time you take a nature walk, watch for daddy longlegs, a harmless long-legged creature related to the spider. Its legs are bent and its body hangs close to the ground. Remember that, like a spider, a daddy longlegs is not an insect—it's an arachnid!

Patterned Butterflies

These beautiful butterflies look like they're made from stained glass! Study the patterns on real butterflies, and see if you can re-create some of them.

What You'll Need:

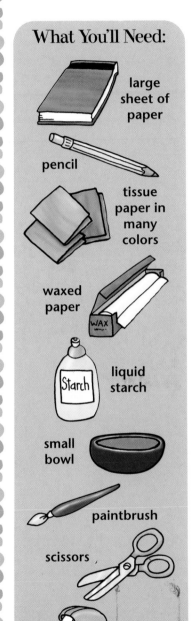

- large sheet of paper
- pencil
- tissue paper in many colors
- waxed paper
- liquid starch
- small bowl
- paintbrush
- scissors
- tape
- butterfly reference books (optional)

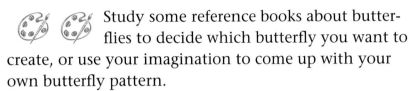 Study some reference books about butterflies to decide which butterfly you want to create, or use your imagination to come up with your own butterfly pattern.

Draw a butterfly outline on a large sheet of paper. Tear sheets of colored tissue paper into different shapes (each shape should measure about 3 inches). Next, place a sheet of waxed paper over the butterfly outline, and pour liquid starch in a small bowl. Use the starch to "paint" the tissue-paper pieces onto the waxed paper, filling in the outline of the butterfly with a mosaic of different colors. Add 1 or 2 more layers of tissue, and allow your butterfly to dry overnight. Cut out the butterfly, following the outline on the underlying paper. Then slowly peel the tissue-paper butterfly off of the waxed paper. Tape your butterfly to the window, and let the sun shine through!

Snow Goggle Giggles

Long ago, people used goggles to fight snow blindness.
You can use them just for fun!

What You'll Need:

egg carton

scissors

string or yarn

decorations
(feathers, sequins, felt)

Tribes that called the frigid arctic regions home had a problem with the brightness of unending snow fields. Too much exposure to the reflection of the sun off the snow could cause blindness, so ancient folks crafted goggles to cut down on the wintery glare. Chances are you don't live in those remote snowy regions, so you can make the goggles just for fun.

Start by cutting 2 sections (one for each eye) out of an egg carton. To attach the sections together at the nose bridge, poke a hole in 1 side of each egg-carton section. Then thread a piece of soft yarn or string through the holes, and tie the 2 ends of yarn together. Next, poke a hole in the other side of each egg-carton section. Attach a string on each side long enough to tie together at the back of your head when you slip the egg cups in place.

Before you put the glasses on, cut small, ½-inch slivers in each egg section. Be sure to keep the cuts narrow so that you can see out with very little reflective light finding its way to your eyes. Decorate the goggles with feathers, string, felt, sequins, or any other decorations you might have around the house. Be careful not to get sequins or other small items in your eyes!

Rock 'n' Paint

Now you can make paint just as people did years ago—with rocks!

What You'll Need:

safety goggles

crumbly rocks and soil

charcoal

big rocks

old bowl

corn syrup

paintbrush

paper

Forget rock 'n' roll. It's time to rock 'n' paint! Make your own paint with materials like rocks, charcoal, and soil.

First, put on safety goggles to protect your eyes. Then gather crumbly rocks, heavy pieces of soil, and charcoal on a big rock. Use another rock to crush the materials into a fine powder. (Watch your fingers!) Believe it or not, this powder will be the base for your paint. Mix the powder in a bowl with a little corn syrup to make a paste-like mixture. Now you're ready to create a masterpiece with your own homemade paint! Just dip a paintbrush into the mixture, and get to work painting on your paper.

Look around your backyard to see what other things can be crushed to make paint and what materials don't work all that well. For example, grass, flowers, leaves, or sticks might be fun to try, but hard rocks won't work too well. See if you can mix different colors that will add some flair to your works of art!

Index